James E. Carter

39th President of the United States

President Jimmy Carter in the Oval Office of the White House one month after his inauguration on January 20, 1977. (Jimmy Carter Library.)

James E. Carter
39th President of the United States

Daniel A. Richman

SS. Colman - John
Neumann Library

 **GARRETT EDUCATIONAL CORPORATION**

Cover: *Official presidential portrait of James E. Carter by Herbert E. Abrams.* (Copyrighted by the White House Historical Association; photograph by the National Geographic Society.)

Edited and produced by Synthegraphics Corporation

Library of Congress Cataloging in Publication Data

Richman, Daniel A., 1953–
  James E. Carter, 39th president of the United States.
  (Presidents of the United States)
  Bibliography: p.
  Includes index.
  Summary: Follows the life of Jimmy Carter, including his childhood, education, employment, political career, and term of presidency.
    1. Carter, Jimmy, 1924–   –Juvenile literature.
  2. Presidents–United States–Biography–Juvenile literature. [1. Carter, Jimmy, 1924–   .
  2. Presidents.] I. Title. II. Title: James E. Carter, thirty-ninth president of the United States. III. Series.
  E873.R53   1989   973.926′092′4–dc19   [B]   [92]
  88-24562
  ISBN 0-944483-24-0

Contents

Chronology for
James E. Carter

1924   Born on October 1 in Plains, Georgia

1943–   Attended the U.S. Naval Academy
1946

1946   Married Rosalynn Smith on July 7

1946–   Served on various assignments as a U.S.
1952   naval officer

1952   Assigned to nuclear submarines under
          Admiral Hyman Rickover

1953–   Resigned from Navy and returned to Plains;
1962   became involved in local civic affairs

1963–   Served in Georgia state senate
1967

1966   Lost Democratic primary race for gover-
          nor of Georgia

1971–   Served as governor of Georgia
1975

1977–   Served as 39th President of the United
1981   States; defeated for re-election to
          presidency by Ronald Reagan; retired to
          Plains

Chapter 1

A Farm Boy from Georgia

"**D**own with America! Down with the great Satan!" A mob of 10,000 Iranians swarmed through the streets of Teheran, Iran, screaming, burning American flags, and hanging banners that read "Death to America Is a Beautiful Thought" and "Khomeini Struggles, Carter Trembles."

Then, after someone with a powerful pair of shears cut through a chain holding closed the metal gates of the American embassy, 500 Iranian students surged into the compound. Donning flak jackets and gas masks, 19 U.S. Marine guards lobbed tear gas grenades into the crowd. The students ripped the masks off the faces of the Marines, shoved them to the ground, and tied their hands. Breaking into the embassy itself, the students seized 62 Americans and took them hostage.

A DIFFICULT PERIOD

President Jimmy Carter had been attending services on that day at Washington's First Baptist Church, as he did every Sunday. It was November 4, 1979—the beginning of what he later called "the most difficult period of my life."

Fourteen months later, 52 Americans were still being held for ransom. The Iranians demanded that the United States return the Shah, who had led the Islamic country until he was forced to flee in January 1979. They also demanded over $540 billion in cash and gold.

Negotiations through the United Nations Security Council had failed. Legal actions through the International Court of Justice in The Hague had failed. A boycott (suspension) of Iranian oil purchases had failed. Through what President Carter called "an incredible series of mishaps," an ambitious rescue attempt in April 1980 had failed, leaving eight U.S. servicemen dead and the wreckage of a helicopter and an airplane burning in the Iranian desert.

Jimmy Carter's term in office was ending. He had risen from a politically unknown Georgia peanut farmer to become the 39th President of the United States by offering Americans openness, honesty, humility, and compassion. But the people wanted effectiveness, too. Though the country rallied around Carter when the hostages were taken, support dwindled as they were held a week, a month—past Thanksgiving and Christmas—for 444 days in all. His loss to Ronald Reagan in the 1980 presidential election was swift and devastating.

At 6:35 on the morning of January 20, 1981—Jimmy Carter's last day as President and Ronald Reagan's first—$7.98 billion of Iran's money that had been frozen in U.S. banks was cabled to Iran's central bank. It was one of the largest financial transactions in history. Six hours later, Flight 133, made up of two Boeing 727s and a small corporate jet, took off from Teheran's airport.

The hostages were on their way home—and so was Jimmy Carter.

GROWING UP BAREFOOT

James Earl Carter, Jr.'s home and childhood were American classics. He was born in a hospital in Plains, Georgia (the first U.S. President to be born in a hospital), on October 1, 1924, and grew up on a 350-acre farm in Archery, Georgia, about two miles west of Plains.

Jimmy and his parents were one of only two permanent white families in Archery. Some poor white families lived there during harvest season, and about 25 black families were also year-round residents. Nearby Plains (population—then and now—about 600) is a center for growing and selling peanuts. Over 24,000 tons of peanuts are grown there every year.

Family Background

Jimmy's father, James Earl Carter, Sr. (called "Earl"), was born in 1894 and grew up on a farm in Arlington, Georgia, 50 miles southwest of Plains. Earl's father, William Archibald Carter, was from Schley County, Georgia, and his mother, Nina Pratt, was born in South Carolina. A farmer and saw-mill owner, William Carter died in 1903 after being shot by his business partner, who was never convicted.

Earl finished 10th grade at a military school, the most education any Carter had received since the family moved to Georgia. Coming to Plains in 1904, Earl became a prominent businessman, buying Plains farmland and timberland and brokering (buying and reselling for a profit) peanuts. He also owned a grocery market and a dry-cleaning store.

Earl met Jimmy's mother, Bessie Lillian Gordy, in Plains when he was 27 and she was 23. The descendant of a Scottish family, Lillian was born in 1898, the fourth of eight nat-

This photograph of Jimmy Carter's parents, Lillian and James Earl Carter, Sr., was taken in 1950. (Charles M. Rafshoon.)

ural children in her family. She moved to Plains from Richland, Georgia, where her father, James Jackson Gordy, had worked as a tax collector and postmaster, to study nursing at Wise Hospital in Plains. After she became a registered nurse, Lillian and Earl were married on September 26, 1923. They lived in Plains until Jimmy was four years old, when they moved to Archery. When Jimmy was two, his sister Gloria was born. Three years later, another sister, Ruth, was born, and eight years later, his brother Billy.

Home and Farm

The Carters' wooden clapboard house in Archery stood alongside a dirt road. It had no electricity, no telephone, and no central heating. To keep Jimmy warm during cold winter nights, his mother would place in his bed several bricks she had heated in one of the house's fireplaces. For part of Jimmy's childhood, there was no running water in the house. Later, a windmill was installed to pump water into the house. Still, water for bathing first had to be heated in a bucket on the kitchen's wood-burning stove. Jimmy wore no shoes from April to October; he wore a shirt only for church or school.

There was no fence around the yard of the Carter home, so chickens, ducks, and geese were able to roam freely. The family also kept mules, horses, sheep, donkeys, goats, cattle, hogs, and milk cows. Following a biblical command, the Carters fed their animals at night before they ate their own dinner.

In addition to its most famous product — peanuts — the farm also produced dairy products, fruits, vegetables, sausages, lard, cured hams, beef, sugar cane syrup, honey, goose feathers (to be put into quilts), wool (to be made up into blankets), and even homemade ketchup made from fresh tomatoes. At his store in Plains, Jimmy's father sold the farm's products as well as other items.

The interior of Earl Carter's store as it appeared in 1925. (Charles M. Rafshoon.)

The family was not wealthy, but it was not poor, either. The lack of conveniences in the Carter home was typical of houses in that time and area. The family made a good income from its farm and store, and Jimmy's father made extra money from brokering peanuts. His mother also worked as a nurse.

HARD WORK, THEN PLAY

Jimmy admired his father as the hardest-working person he had ever known. That admiration kept him from complaining about his own constant hard work and from ever refusing to do it. As Jimmy later wrote, "Daddy would say to me, 'Hot ("Hot Shot" is what he called me), Hot, would you like to turn the potato vines this afternoon?' And I would much rather go to the movie or something. But I always said, 'Yes, sir, Daddy, I would.' And I would do it." Jimmy saw his father as "a very firm but understanding director of my life and habits" and "always my best friend."

The work went on from dawn to dark, all year 'round. Along with other boys who lived nearby, all of whom were black, Jimmy brought water in buckets from a spring to older field workers, carried stove wood, gathered eggs, carried slop to the hogs, milked cows, and sheared sheep. The job he disliked most was coating each cotton bud with a mixture of arsenic, molasses, and water. This was done to kill boll weevils, insects that would destroy the crop. After awhile, his trousers, legs, and bare feet dripped with the syrupy goo, attracting clouds of flies. At night, he had to stand his trousers in the corner of the room because the knees would not bend.

Every Sunday, the Carter children attended services and Sunday school at Plains Baptist Church, the town's biggest.

But Jimmy's mother usually stayed home, and his father often skipped the service and went to the drug store to talk with friends.

Hunting and Fishing

When he was not working, Jimmy loved to hunt and fish. Those activities were a normal part of life, partly because meat was scarce during the Great Depression (a period of severe poverty in the 1930s), but mostly because of tradition. With other boys and their fathers, Jimmy and his father hunted for raccoon, squirrels, and quail.

Jimmy's favorite fishing partner was Rachel Clark, a black girl who could outfish anyone in the neighborhood. Jimmy had to earn his right to fish with her by digging earthworms or finding caterpillars. They would walk as far as five miles from the farm to catch catfish and largemouth bass in Choctawhatchee or Kinchafoonee Creek.

Segregation: A Way of Life

All but one of Jimmy's playmates were black, and his best friend was, too. Lillian treated black patients in their homes, and Earl visited black farm workers to discuss crops and the weather. Sometimes black and white churches in Plains would hold worship services and picnics together.

Still, blacks were segregated (kept apart) from whites. They had to attend separate schools and churches, could not ride the schoolbus, sat separately on the train, did not visit white people's houses, were expected to lose at children's games, and were buried in separate cemeteries. "Our lives were dominated by unspoken, unwritten, but powerful rules, rules that were almost never challenged," Jimmy said later.

A LOVE FOR BOOKS

Though Jimmy's father rarely read, Jimmy loved books, as did his mother. He especially liked adventure books by Zane Grey and Jack London, nature books by John Muir, and hunting and fishing magazines.

Julia Coleman ran the Plains school Jimmy attended from the first grade through high school, from which he graduated in June 1941 at the age of 16. She encouraged her students to learn about music, art, and especially literature. Every student was required to debate, memorize and recite long poems and chapters from the Bible, and learn to play a musical instrument.

When Jimmy was 12, "Miss Julia" told him he was ready to read *War and Peace.* He was happy because he thought it was about cowboys and Indians. When he checked it out of the library, he was shocked to find it was 1,400 pages long and about the French army's defeat in Russia under the emperor Napoleon. In time, it became one of his favorite books, because it is about how common, ordinary people – students, farmers, barbers, housewives – affect history.

Jimmy also enjoyed sports. He played tennis on the court next to his house (one of only four tennis courts in Plains). While he was in high school, his favorite sports were baseball, basketball, and track.

AN EARLY DOSE OF POLITICS

Jimmy was exposed to politics when he was very young. His father served for many years on the Sumter County School Board and was one of the first directors of a federal program that brought electricity to Jimmy's house when he was 13 years old.

Electricity made it possible to do lots of work around the farm quicker and easier. It also made it possible to carry on activities at night. As farmers began to meet in the evenings to discuss electricity and other matters of local interest, the Carters got to know others from throughout the county and the region. And as their concerns increasingly expanded beyond their family to the outside world, Earl became more involved in politics. He was even elected to the Georgia state legislature and served for a year before he died in 1953. Earl encouraged Jimmy to attend rallies for local politicians, which Jimmy did and enjoyed.

Jimmy's childhood traits hint at the kind of man he would become: he was a hard worker, he was self-disciplined and philosophical, he valued knowledge and honesty, and he loved nature. Other qualities he has as a man that were not evident in his childhood include his deep religious belief, his leadership abilities, his political ambition, and his hatred of racial inequality.

Chapter 2

"Why Not the Best?"

Jimmy dripped with cold sweat. He was sitting alone in a large room with Admiral Hyman G. Rickover, being interviewed for a position in Rickover's program to design and build America's first atomic-powered submarines. Jimmy, then 27 and a lieutenant, wanted the assignment more than any other in the Navy.

For over two hours, Rickover had been asking Jimmy impossibly difficult questions on topics that Jimmy himself had chosen. He always looked right into Jimmy's eyes, and he never smiled. Finally, Rickover shot out a question that Jimmy thought he could answer well.

"How did you stand in your class at the Naval Academy?" Rickover asked.

"Sir, I stood 59th in a class of 820!" Jimmy replied proudly, awaiting congratulations that never came.

"Did you do your best?" Rickover asked.

Jimmy started to say "Yes, sir," but then he recalled some of the many times he could have learned more about America's allies, enemies, weapons, and strategies. He finally gulped and said, "No, sir, I didn't *always* do my best."

Rickover looked at Jimmy a long time, then swiveled in his chair to end the interview. With his back turned, Rickover posed one final question: "Why not?" he asked.

Jimmy sat there awhile, shaken, and then slowly left the room. Rickover's question was one that Jimmy would think about his whole life. He even used it as the title of his autobiography, *Why Not the Best?* The man who had asked this question influenced him more than anyone in his life, except his parents.

AT ANNAPOLIS

As a child, Jimmy had loved getting letters and souvenirs sent from faraway places by his uncle, Tom Gordy, who was in the Navy. From the age of six, Jimmy had wanted to attend the U.S. Naval Academy in Annapolis, Maryland, and worried constantly as he was growing up that he would not be accepted. If he were, he would be the first Carter to attend college. Graduating from Annapolis would allow him easier entry into politics, law, or finance, and the U.S. government would pay part of his expenses.

Jimmy did get accepted, but before going to Annapolis he attended junior college at Georgia Southwestern in Americus, just a few miles from Plains, for one year. He then transferred to Georgia Institute of Technology the next year, where he joined the Navy ROTC (Reserve Officers' Training Corps) and studied general engineering, seamanship, and navigation. He finished the year in the top 10 percent of his class and made the honor roll.

Life as a Plebe

In June 1943, when he was 18 years old, Jimmy left Georgia for the first time to attend the Naval Academy. Because World War II was going on and the country needed naval officers, the normal four-year course at Annapolis was condensed into three years. In addition to his homesickness, as a "plebe" (first-year student) Jimmy had to endure constant demands for songs, poems, reports, and speeches from seniors (third-year students). Punishment for an inadequate performance—or for bad table manners or even for odd facial expressions—was a beating with brooms or serving spoons, running an obstacle course in the dark, extra marching, or loss of free time.

The Navy tolerated this traditional "hazing" in the belief that it toughened and tested the men. Although Jimmy suffered his share, he said he "refused to take it seriously and treated it as a game."

The Annapolis schedule imposed strict discipline. Students awoke to a bugle call at 6:15 A.M. and had to be out of bed with room doors opened within 40 seconds. Lights had to be out by 10:00 P.M., and from morning to night every minute of the day was filled with activity.

Every student had the same courses: gunnery, seamanship, navigation, astronomy, engineering, naval tactics, and a foreign language. Jimmy chose Spanish for his foreign language. Although it was impossible to complete all regular assignments, Jimmy thought a broader education was important, so he privately studied literature, philosophy, theology, and music. He and his roommate also enjoyed classical records. And just before dinner each day, Jimmy worked out for the school's cross-country team and drilled for its football team. While at the Naval Academy, he even learned to fly airplanes.

In his senior year, Jimmy received instruction in after-dinner speaking and ballroom dancing. At the academy proms, held twice a month, the students practiced their dancing skills and etiquette (formal manners).

Jimmy scored 96 out of a possible 110 points his first

Jimmy was 22 years old and a midshipman at the U.S. Naval Academy when he gave this photo to his fiancée, Rosalynn Smith. (Columbus Ledger-Enquirer.)

year at Annapolis and graduated 60th (not 59th, as he later told Admiral Rickover) in his class. Even though he described his years at the academy as "a time of challenge," he received his good grades without much effort. He had a reputation for cheerfulness and friendliness. He did not smoke, drink, or swear. Yet his classmates recalled that he did not stand out as a leader in his class or even among the 100 or so men who made up his "company," the academy's basic social unit.

Jimmy and Rosalynn

Before going to Annapolis, Jimmy had dated two or three girls but had never had a serious girl friend. Then, when he came home from the academy during a break in the summer of 1944 dressed in his gleaming white uniform, a friend of his sister Ruth noticed him. Jimmy was 20 at the time; Ruth's friend, Rosalynn Smith, also a Plains resident, was 17. After their first date, a movie, Jimmy's mother asked what he thought of her. He told her, "She's the girl I want to marry."

During his Christmas vacation the next year, Jimmy saw "Roz" every night. They were married on July 7, 1946, in Plains, a month after his graduation from Annapolis. Today, he calls her "a full partner in every sense of the word. . . . We [have] been ridiculed at times for allowing our love to be apparent to others. It was not an affectation [an act], but was as natural as breathing."

ON—AND UNDER—THE SEA

After graduating from Annapolis, Jimmy, now a naval officer, was assigned to the *Wyoming*, a converted old battleship. Every week, the ship would leave its home port of Norfolk,

Virginia, carrying experimental navigation, radar, communications, and gunnery equipment to be tested at sea. Jimmy was responsible for analyzing how the new equipment performed.

Because he spent so much time at sea, Jimmy seldom saw Rosalynn. During his 11 years in the Navy, that would be the norm. He described his life with Rosalynn then as one of "constant separations interspersed with ecstatic reunions and the melding of ourselves over the years into a closer relationship of love, understanding, and mutual respect." Their first child, John ("Jack") William, was born on July 3, 1947, in Portsmouth, Virginia.

After serving his required two years on surface ships, Jimmy chose submarines for his next assignment. The family moved to New London, Connecticut, where he spent six months in training. He learned almost by heart a submarine's complex fuel, water, hydraulic, air, electrical, and mechanical systems.

Aboard the *Pomfret*

In December 1948, Rosalynn and Jack went back to Plains while Jimmy went to Hawaii, where he was assigned to duty on board the submarine *Pomfret*. His first trip was to China, and it was extremely rough. During one of the worst storms in history to hit the Pacific Ocean, Jimmy was seasick for five straight days. One night, while standing watch on the bridge about 15 feet above the ocean, a wave tore Jimmy's hand from the railing and knocked him to the deck. The current carried him backward about 30 feet, where he landed on top of a gun. If the current had been different, he would have been lost at sea.

The *Pomfret* made trips out of Pearl Harbor for 1½ years, often serving as a target in the Yellow Sea so American and British surface ships could practice their antisubmarine tactics. In April 1949, Jack and Rosalynn joined Jimmy in Hawaii, where she gave birth to their second son, James Earl ("Chip") Carter, III, on April 12, 1950. The *Pomfret* was transferred back to San Diego that month, and the growing Carter family followed.

Shortly thereafter, they moved again, this time back to New London, Connecticut. The Navy had decided to build its first new ship since the end of World War II, the USS *K-1,* an ultraquiet submarine designed to fight other submarines underwater. Jimmy represented the U.S. Navy during construction, making sure the experimental equipment being installed, such as the long-range sonar, worked properly. If it did not, he would help redesign it. When the ship was finished, Jimmy served aboard it through October 1952. The Carters' third son, Donnel Jeffrey, was born on August 18 of that year.

WORKING WITH RICKOVER

It was while on the *K-1* that Jimmy was interviewed by Admiral Rickover. Despite Jimmy's admission about not "doing his best," he was accepted into Rickover's nuclear submarine program. For four months he worked at the Atomic Energy Commission in Washington, D.C. Then, in March 1953, Jimmy and his family moved to Schenectady, New York, where the *Sea Wolf,* one of two experimental atomic submarines, was to be built.

Jimmy studied reactor engine technology and nuclear

physics at a nearby college. Then, as the *Sea Wolf*'s senior officer, he taught those topics to his men. He also assisted in building the new submarine's reactor.

Jimmy's experience in the atomic submarine program was important to him because it gave him the opportunity to work with Admiral Rickover. Rickover's nuclear submarines would eventually revolutionize the American Navy. But when he first proposed such submarines in the 1940s, his ideas were fought or ignored. Then he was passed over twice for promotion in the early 1950s, which, in the Navy, means forced retirement. Only the direct action of President Truman saved his career. Jimmy admired Rickover's perseverance in the face of obstacles. He also admired Truman's ability to recognize Rickover's outstanding qualities, and Truman's courage in standing up for Rickover.

Rickover demanded total dedication from his men. He expected them to know their jobs down to the smallest detail. If a job was not done to his satisfaction, he never hesitated to criticize, but he never praised a job that was well done. "The absence of comment was his compliment," Jimmy remembers. Regarding his relationship with Rickover, Jimmy also remembers:

> If he found no fault, he simply looked, turned around, and walked away. However, if I had made the slightest mistake, in one of the loudest and most obnoxious voices I ever heard, he would turn around and tell the other people in the area what a horrible disgrace I was to the Navy, and that I ought to be back in the oldest and slowest and smallest submarine from which I had come.

Despite Rickover's manner, Jimmy and his men respected him and tried as hard as they could to please him. That was because he was "unbelievably hard-working and competent," Jimmy said. He called him "probably the most competent and innovative naval engineer of all time." As Jimmy's father had, Rickover "expected the maximum from us, but he always contributed more." Jimmy said Rickover knew more about constructing ships than the shipbuilders did.

As a politician, Jimmy tried to work as hard as his hero had. But unlike Rickover, he was careful to compliment those who had done a good job, often sending a handwritten note.

BACK TO PLAINS

Jimmy's visits home were rare. During one, his growing awareness of the evil of racism caused an argument with his father, who, although he acted kindly toward blacks, still believed in segregation. Jimmy told his father the story about a visit the *K-1* made to Nassau in 1950. The ship's crew had accepted an invitation to attend a party. At the last minute, a message arrived saying that, according to Bahamian custom, only white crew members could attend the party. In support of the ship's one black sailor, the entire crew skipped the event. Earl could not understand why, and the discussion grew so heated that he and Jimmy agreed to avoid race as a topic in the future.

Despite their differences, in the summer of 1953, when Jimmy heard that the cancer from which his father was suffering was becoming worse, he took a leave from the Navy and went home to Plains. Before Earl died on July 22 at the age of 59, hundreds of people came by to see him. Jimmy was struck by his father's obvious importance to the community, fostered by his wide range of activities and interests. When Jimmy compared his own life to that of his father's, he felt that it lacked roots. After days of "torturous" thought, he decided to return to Plains. That winter, Jimmy, Rosalynn, and their three young sons left the Navy and went back to Georgia.

A Life of Service

While in the Navy, Jimmy sometimes visited the U.S. senators from Georgia when he was in Washington on duty. Overall, though, he had little contact with politics during his Navy years. "When I was at Annapolis, the only thing I wanted to be was chief of naval operations," he said later.

By 1953, however, when he returned to Plains, the idea of a political career had begun to take hold. "I had only one life to live, and I wanted to live it as a civilian, with a potentially fuller opportunity for varied public service," he said.

Jimmy Carter's climb toward the presidency was about to begin.

Chapter 3

From Farm to State Senate

For the second time in a week, two organizers from the White Citizen's Council had come to call.

"Every man in this town has joined up except you," the police chief said. "You wouldn't want to be the only hold-out, would you?"

"It *could* damage your reputation – and your business," the Baptist preacher added. "We'll loan you the money if you can't afford the $5 in dues." Several of Jimmy Carter's close friends, who had already been recruited by the organizers, nodded their heads in agreement.

The council was one of many that had sprung up throughout the South in response to a 1954 Supreme Court ruling *(Brown v. Board of Education)* which said that separate but equal public schools are inherently (basically) unequal and thus violate the highest law of the land, the Constitution. Segregation in the South and everywhere else in the country was threatened – and so were the many who supported it.

Jimmy stared at the men. They offended his principles. "It's not a question of the money," he said. "I told you before:

After leaving the Navy, Jimmy returned to Plains, where he became a peanut farmer. (Charles M. Rafshoon.)

I have no intention of joining your organization, now or ever. And if necessary, I'll leave Plains to avoid you."

The council then organized a boycott against Jimmy's struggling peanut company, but the boycott failed. That incident was only one of many times that Jimmy Carter would stand up and fight against racial inequality.

BACK ON THE FARM

Returning to farming after so many years in the Navy was difficult for Jimmy. Nevertheless, he took courses in agriculture, read books about farming, and talked to other farmers.

Jimmy and his mother formed a partnership and started a company to grow improved peanut seeds, with Jimmy as the company's only employee. The partnership, which made less than $200 in its first year, took over Earl's business of growing and storing peanuts in Carter's Warehouse. Later, Jimmy's younger brother, Billy, also became a partner.

In their second year back in Plains, Rosalynn started coming to the office once a week. Before long, she became Jimmy's full-time work partner. Later, they bought a cotton gin and began to process cotton for farmers.

Jimmy, Rosalynn, and the children lived in a public housing project for their first few months in Plains, then they moved into a rented house. In 1956, as business improved, they moved to a house in Archery, the town where Jimmy had grown up. Then, in 1961, the Carters built a bungalow in the woods on the edge of Plains.

Their oldest son, Jack, was six when the family returned to Plains. He went to first grade in the same school that his father had attended.

"Hey, Get Your Fresh Groundpeas Here!"

Shouldn't that be "fresh *peanuts*"? Yes, but peanuts—also known as goobers, goober peas, and pindas—are actually peas, not nuts, and groundpeas is another proper name for them.

Jimmy Carter's home state of Georgia grows more peanuts than any other. In 1987 it grew nearly half the country's total—over 790,000 tons.

Early Americans fed the peanuts to pigs. It was not until around 1920 that peanuts became a major crop. Now, most of them are used for food. Enjoyed throughout the world for their taste, they are also a healthy nutrient, with more protein than an equal weight of steak.

Peanut oil, made from pressing peanuts, is used in soap, paint, and nitroglycerin, an explosive. What's left after the peanuts are pressed makes a good food for animals. Even peanut shells have a use: when ground into powder, they are mixed into plastic and wallboard.

The "pioneer of peanuts" was George Washington Carver, born in 1864 to a Missouri slave woman. In 1896, Carver was drawn to Alabama's Tuskegee Institute (now Tuskegee University) by the speeches of its founder, Booker T. Washington, who believed that education, not political agitation, served the best interests of blacks.

As the head of Tuskegee's Research

Through his discoveries, George Washington Carver, a black scientist at Tuskegee Institute in Alabama, made the peanut a major agricultural crop in the South. (Library of Congress.)

Department, Carver devoted his life to research aimed at improving southern agriculture. When he went to Tuskegee after attending college in Iowa, peanuts were not considered an important crop in the South or anywhere else. But within 50 years after Carver arrived at Tuskegee, they were the South's second largest cash crop (after cotton). Carver's research developed more than 300 products from peanuts, as well as more than 100 from sweet potatoes. He also researched and promoted soil conservation and crop diversification.

Although Carver became internationally known for his work, he remained a humble, gentle man until his death in 1943. For his efforts he was honored by both the U.S. and foreign governments. He left his life savings of $33,000 to Tuskegee Institute.

First Step into Politics

Though the now-flourishing business kept him busy, Jimmy began to get more involved in civic affairs, joining several organizations and becoming a member of the Sumter County School Board. After a careful study, in 1961 the board recommended that some of the county's high schools be closed and others expanded to save money in upkeep and salaries. Jimmy (by then chairman) made speeches around the county in support of the proposal, encountering bitter opposition from his Plains neighbors, who stood to lose one of their schools. When the proposal was defeated, Jimmy found it a "stinging disappointment."

But the defeat was not painful enough to discourage Jimmy. The next year, in a discussion with a visiting minister after evening services, he declared that he was considering running for public office. The pastor strongly advised Jimmy to avoid a profession with such a poor reputation. "If you want to be of service, why don't you go into the ministry or into some honorable social service work?" he asked.

Jimmy replied, "How would *you* like to be the pastor of a church with 80,000 members?" The pastor finally admitted it might be possible to stay honest and still serve the needs of the 80,000 citizens in the 14th senate district, where the Carters lived.

At the last minute, in September 1962, Jimmy decided to run for a state senate seat.

A WHIRLWIND CAMPAIGN

With the enthusiastic help of his family and close friends, Jimmy mounted an "amateurish, whirlwind" campaign. Most of his supporters were young and inexperienced in politics. His opponent in the Democratic primary election (to choose which Democrat would run against the Republican candidate in the general election) was an experienced politician, as were many of the opponent's backers.

On election day, Jimmy visited as many polling places as he could. In all but Georgetown, a small town at the district's edge, proper voting procedures were being followed. There, voters had to mark their ballots on a table, with officials watching, instead of privately in booths. As they did, the supervisor would point to Jimmy's opponent's campaign material on the table and say, "This is a good man, and my friend." Sometimes he reached into the ballot box and pulled out ballots to be sure they were marked "properly."

When the polls closed, the Georgetown ballot box contained 420 ballots, even though only 333 people had officially received them. Many clumps of four to eight ballots were folded together, and at least 125 people seemed to have voted in alphabetical order.

Jimmy worked with a friend and a local lawyer to investigate the fraud. His life was threatened several times, and the local newspapers called him naive and a poor loser. His opponent was declared the winner.

Jimmy then called a reporter at a bigger newspaper, the *Atlanta Constitution,* who focused statewide attention on the fraud. In his fight to reverse the decision, Jimmy "nearly memorized the state election laws." After three frantic weeks of legal challenges, a court declared him the primary's winner. He then won the general election by 1,500 votes, after which he went to bed sick and exhausted. The corrupt supervisor in Georgetown was later convicted for vote fraud.

In the State Senate

Jimmy's hard work did not end when he won the campaign for state senator. It had just begun. He promised himself he would read every bill before voting on it. That meant reading 800 to 1,000 bills — some short, others 300 pages long — during each session. The sessions lasted only 40 days, and there would be one session during each of the four years in his term.

When Jimmy arrived in Atlanta in January 1963, he would go to the State Capitol building early every morning just to read bills. By working those extra hours and taking a speed-reading course, he was able to keep his promise to read all bills before voting on them.

Jimmy also took particular interest in several specific topics. One was equal education for all citizens. With marches, demonstrations, and lawsuits, the civil rights movement had come to the South. But progress in eliminating segregation was slow. Two years earlier, the Reverend Martin Luther King, Jr., had been arrested and jailed in Americus after leading a freedom march. Many of Georgia's education laws tried to retain segregation. But in the growing spirit of integration, Jimmy helped write a law to provide better and more equal education for all Georgia students.

Jimmy was also especially interested in voting rights and election laws. In his first speech to the state senate, he attacked the "30 Questions" that blacks for generations had been required to answer correctly before they could register to vote. The questions were so difficult that even the people asking them did not know the right answers. In 1964, the state legislature passed a law eliminating some of the questions. That same law also made changes in how elections must be conducted, mainly because of the corruption during Jimmy's senate race.

Fighting the Special Interests

Another great concern of Jimmy's was learning how the state government worked—and why it did not work better. Early in his term as a state senator, he noticed that many legislators introduced bills that favored "special interests"—that is, certain individuals or groups. For example, the more some Georgia employees worked to help legislators pass certain bills, the more often those legislators passed bills giving the employees pay raises.

Jimmy quickly became disgusted with special-interest bills. He also came to detest lobbyists, the people who pushed the legislators to pass their special-interest bills. He realized that lobbyists are not immoral or illegal. They simply represent "the most selfish aspect of the character of their clients," who might be doctors, lawyers, bankers, or any other group wanting a certain bill passed. Often, what lobbyists want for their employers is not what is best for the general public.

By yielding to lobbyists, the senators were not acting responsibly, Jimmy thought. And because they often made their decisions in meetings behind closed doors, they were not representing the people who had voted for them.

Jimmy tried to eliminate the pay increases to state employees, but he did not succeed. Nevertheless, he continued to fight special interests and closed meetings for his entire political career.

Trying to Simplify

The new senator found the Georgia government "almost unbelievably" confused and complicated. Once a program or agency was created, it usually existed forever, growing slowly and surely, "like a fungus." Jimmy found that some legislators liked the confusion, because it let them conceal their special privileges and avoid responsibility. His attempts to simplify and reorganize the state government were unsuccessful, but those goals, too, would remain important in his political future.

During his four years in the state senate, Jimmy had time to see and think about how government works. Although he disliked much of what he saw, he still thought public service was important, and he formed strong feelings about which issues were most important. Even though he lost some battles, he enjoyed enough successes for his colleagues to name him one of the senate's five most effective legislators.

Chapter 4

Down but Not Out

Jimmy had lost 22 pounds. He was depressed, tired, and deeply in debt. "Everything I did was not gratifying," he said. "When I succeeded in something, I got no pleasure out of it. When I failed at something, it was a horrible experience for me."

It was early in 1967. After three months of frantic campaigning to become the Democratic nominee for governor of Georgia, Jimmy had lost—badly. Lester Maddox, a racist restaurant owner who once had brandished a pistol on his restaurant's front steps to ward off black customers, had won the primary election.

One day, while walking with his sister, Ruth Carter Stapleton, Jimmy asked her, "You and I are both Baptists, but what is it that you have that I haven't got?"

She said, "Jimmy, through my hurt and pain I finally got so bad off I had to forget everything I was. What it amounts to in religious terms is total commitment. I belong to Jesus, everything I am."

Jimmy said, "Ruth, that's what I want."

"Would you give up anything for Christ? Your life, your possessions—everything?" Ruth asked.

"I would," Jimmy said.

"Would you be willing to give up politics?"

Jimmy thought for a long time. Then he had to admit that he would not.

FIRST RACE FOR GOVERNOR

It had been in March 1966 that, while still a state senator, Jimmy had decided to run for the U.S. Congress. Huge social and civil rights programs, like the Civil Rights Act of 1964, had been enacted by the country's Democratic-controlled Congress and by Democratic President Lyndon B. Johnson. Now, Republican candidates who opposed those programs were gaining strength in the South for the first time since the Civil War. Although Barry Goldwater, a Republican senator from Arizona, had failed in his challenge to defeat incumbent (current office-holder) Lyndon Johnson for the presidency in 1964, he had carried Georgia and several other southern states.

Partly out of loyalty to the Democrats (but mostly out of his own political ambition), Jimmy decided to challenge the incumbent U.S. congressman from his district, a Republican named Bo Callaway. Callaway, however, withdrew from the congressional race and entered the race for governor. That gave Jimmy an excellent chance to win Callaway's congressional seat. But because Jimmy also regarded Callaway as a personal rival, he, too, quit the congressional race and announced for governor.

Jimmy had only three months to campaign before the Democratic primary election. Like his campaign for state senator, the one for governor was "intensive and frantic." Furthermore, he now had to campaign throughout the state rather than just in one small district. Carter was so unknown that some journalists labeled him "Jimmy *Who?*" He, Rosalynn, Lillian, and his sons split up and campaigned for 16 to 18 hours a day throughout Georgia. Among them, they met more than 300,000 citizens.

At that time, Hamilton Jordan, who would later manage Jimmy's 1976 presidential campaign and be appointed his chief aide, was a political science major at the University of Georgia. He joined the campaign after Jimmy appeared on campus. Jody Powell, who would later serve as news director during the 1976 presidential campaign and press secretary during Jimmy's presidency, also joined the campaign.

Jimmy finished last of three candidates in the Democratic primary. Lester Maddox, who won the primary, later defeated Bo Calloway for governor.

BORN AGAIN

It was the loss in the Democratic primary that led to Jimmy's conversation with his sister Ruth. At about the same time, the pastor in his Plains church gave a sermon entitled "If you were arrested for being a Christian, would there be enough evidence to convict you?" Jimmy came to the sobering realization that he could probably have talked his way out of the charge.

After these experiences, Jimmy worked toward developing a "more intimate relationship with Christ." He said:

> . . . The first time we're born as children, it's human life given to us; and when we accept Jesus as our Savior it's a new life. That's what "born again" means.
>
> I was baptized when I was 11 years old [but] I never did have a personal feeling of intimacy with Christ until, I'd say

[1964 or 1966], and then I began to see much more clearly the significance of Christ in my life, and it changed my attitudes dramatically. . . . I became much more deeply committed to study and using my example to explain to other people about Christ.

With other churchgoers, Jimmy started making annual "missionary trips" within and outside Georgia, visiting and talking with other Christians. On one such trip, Jimmy spent several days working among Spanish-speaking ghetto residents in Springfield, Massachusetts. "Since then, I've had just about like a new life," Jimmy said later. "As far as hatreds, frustrations, I feel at ease with myself."

Jimmy's faith gave him an enormous sense of self-confidence and security. He has no doubt about his faith and no doubt about the purpose of his life. "I feel at ease with myself," he said. "And it doesn't mean that I'm better [than others], but I'm better off myself."

"SHOW ME A LOSER . . ."

Jimmy had told Ruth he would not give up politics because he did not think his political ambitions conflicted with service to God. "I . . . have a conviction that whatever talent God gave me should be used to the maximum degree," he said. "I believe God wants me to be the best politician I can possibly be."

True to his word, only a month after losing the Democratic primary race, he launched his campaign for the governor's election in 1970. This time, with four years in which to work, he was determined to win. "You show me a good loser and I will show you a loser," he said.

Jimmy set about at once working "with more concentration and commitment than ever before in my life." On a typical day, he would go to his warehouse or farm early in the morning, after which he would work and perform civic duties until late afternoon. Then he would drive somewhere in Georgia to make a speech, returning home late at night. On the way home, he would dictate into a tape recorder the names of people he had met and information about the community in which he had just spoken. The next day, Rosalynn would write thank-you notes on an automatic typewriter that recorded the people's names, addresses, and coded descriptions for use in the future.

A group of young volunteers helped Jimmy prepare charts and graphs that showed, for each of Georgia's 159 counties, how people had voted on various issues and which candidates they had supported. This helped Jimmy plan his platform (his political position on important issues) and analyze the platform of his opponents.

Amidst all the hubbub, a daughter, Amy Lynn Carter, was born, on October 19, 1967.

Winning the Governorship

As the election approached, Jimmy stepped up his efforts. He made about 1,800 speeches in total and shook hands with more than 600,000 people. During the last few months, he and Rosalynn each met at least three factory shifts a day. They usually split up so they could meet more people.

Between them, Rosalynn and Jimmy shook hands with entire crowds at high school football games, livestock and tobacco barns, and rodeos. Then they visited every barber shop, beauty parlor, restaurant, store, and service station in the town. They also visited isolated country radio stations, where the announcer was often so lonely he was happy to interview them. Jimmy made a point of seeing both the black and white communities in the towns he visited and of using black volunteers.

Because money was tight, no one in the campaign stayed in hotels. Instead, they would stay overnight with supporters, engaging in late-night talks that cemented friendships in outlying towns all over the state.

Jimmy's Democratic opponent in the primary election was former Governor Carl B. Sanders, who won most of the state's newspapers' and politicians' endorsements (public declarations of approval). But in the primary election in September 1970, Jimmy beat Sanders. Then, in the general election the next month, he beat the Republican candidate, Hal Suit, winning nearly 60 percent of the vote and carrying almost all of Georgia's counties.

Chapter 5

A Bold Governor

When Jimmy Carter was inaugurated (sworn in) as governor on January 12, 1971, he said, "I believe I know our people as well as anyone. Based on this knowledge of Georgians . . . I say to you quite frankly that the time for racial discrimination is over."

EQUALITY, JUSTICE, AND NATURE

As one of his major goals for the state of Georgia, Jimmy wanted to give "poor, rural, weak, or black" citizens an equal opportunity for education, justice, and employment. During his term as governor, Jimmy appointed dozens of blacks to the board of directors of the state welfare department, the prison system, the university system, and other boards and agencies. He also gave a judgeship to a black lawyer who just a few years before had been denied admission to Georgia Law School because of his color.

When Jimmy came into office, only three blacks had been appointed to leadership positions in the Georgia state government. When he left, there were 53, and the number of black government employees had grown by 30 percent.

In trying to improve his state's criminal justice system, Jimmy helped pass laws creating better ways of choosing, disciplining, and removing judges. Despite his many efforts, he

Jimmy Carter served as governor of Georgia from 1971 to 1975. (Charles M. Rafshoon.)

never succeeded in reducing the number of prisoners in Georgia jails. However, by the end of his term, there were four times more educational programs in prisons, more than twice as many treatment programs, and more than four times as many professional counselors working with prisoners than there had been when he was elected governor.

Working to protect "the weak" with Rosalynn's help, Jimmy set up 130 community centers throughout the state to better care for the mentally ill, who were a special concern of Rosalynn's.

Watching Butterflies

Despite his heavy responsibilities, Jimmy still cherished nature, just as he had while growing up. One day, he and his family lay on their backs on the lawn outside the governor's mansion to watch millions of monarch butterflies migrating southward to Mexico. Because he cared so much for nature, another of Jimmy's concerns as governor was protecting the state's environment. He fought, though unsuccessfully, against the building of a dam on the Flint River. And he worked toward buying unspoiled stretches of land along the Chattahoochee River outside Atlanta to preserve them as wilderness. He also created an organization to buy and protect historical buildings and sites in the state.

Jimmy tried to attract industry to Georgia, which created jobs. But he made it clear that "we don't want you as a new neighbor if you come here looking for cheap labor, special tax privileges, or the right to spoil our environment."

Jimmy also wanted to give people the feeling that the government was open and responsive to them. To do so, he opened his office once a month to anyone who wanted to come without an appointment and ask questions or make requests, suggestions, or criticisms. He called these days "a very instructive and helpful ordeal."

REORGANIZING THE STATE GOVERNMENT

Jimmy's most important goal as governor was to reorganize Georgia's government. When he came into office, there were 300 state agencies, many of which did the same thing. "Every time I open a closet door in my office, I fear that a new state agency will fall out!" he said. Seven agencies worked on educating deaf children, and 22 were responsible for the use of water. The agencies all asked for more money every year, but except in the case of new agencies, no one checked to make sure their programs were worth paying for.

Jimmy helped put together a reorganization bill to shrink the number of agencies. Part of the bill was a plan called zero-based budgeting. According to this plan, every program in every state agency would first be analyzed to be sure it was necessary. Once that was done, every year each program would start out with no money and would have to give good reasons why it should receive any. With his bill, Jimmy hoped to make the government easier for people to deal with, less expensive, and more efficient.

"He . . . Pushes and Pushes"

The reaction to Jimmy's bill by Georgia's legislators, appointees, and employees — and by special-interest groups — was not always enthusiastic. Many of them were interested only in keeping the power and privileges they had under the current way the government operated.

Getting your way as a politician often means compromising — giving up one goal to achieve another. Jimmy hated the kind of compromising most often used in the state legislature: getting legislators to support him in return for his support of bills favoring them, their friends, or their constituents (the people they represented), sometimes at the expense of the general public. Some parts of Jimmy's reorganization bill had to be sacrificed because he would not make the necessary compromises.

Jimmy was stubborn in pushing his bill. One state official said, "Carter reminds me of a South Georgia turtle. He doesn't go around a log. He just sticks his head in the middle and pushes and pushes until the log gives way."

Bringing Pressure to Bear

Beyond his own pushing, Jimmy knew that to get his bill passed, he would have to get citizens to put pressure on their unmotivated legislators to back the plan. He strongly publicized the bill and held 51 public meetings around the state. At these meetings he encouraged people to express their ideas and feelings on what the government should do about mental and physical health, taxes, education, welfare, prisons, criminal justice, the environment, and other issues. He sometimes moved the entire legislature to a small town to give people a better idea of how their state government works. (Of course, during those sessions he would discuss how his reorganization bill would make state government work even better!)

In March 1972, Jimmy's reorganization bill became law, with almost all of the provisions he had pushed for. The number of state agencies was reduced from 300 to 22. By 1975, when Jimmy left office, the state budget was $10 million less than the year before, and the state had an extra $200 million in its treasury. Not everyone agreed that the reorganization bill was a success, but it was Jimmy's greatest accomplishment yet.

A Good Job

Though Jimmy's stubbornness irritated many legislators, most people thought he was doing a good job as governor. He would get to his office by 7:15 every morning and often would work late into the night. But Jimmy loved the work, never getting up "without looking forward to the day with great anticipation." People who worked with him said he was extremely intelligent and could master tremendous amounts of detail. He described his governorship as being "highly controversial, aggressive, and combative."

Jimmy could have added "compassionate" and "responsible." Those qualities were encouraged by his religious beliefs. "The sad duty of politics is to establish justice in a sinful world," he said, quoting a noted theologian. He spent "much time in prayer on [his] knees in the back room of the governor's office."

Jimmy's achievements gained him some fame. His face smiled out from the cover of *Time* magazine in May 1971, and the story inside saluted his integration efforts.

PLANNING FOR THE PRESIDENCY

While in the Navy, Jimmy had once seen President Truman at a distance. He viewed him "with reverence and awe." While he was governor, he met President Nixon and many men who wanted to become President. After meeting them, he lost his awe.

Feeling competent to run for President became "a whole lot easier" when Jimmy started comparing his own experience and knowledge against those of other presidential hopefuls. He began to feel he was "as qualified to be President as any one of them."

In December 1972, Jimmy called his family together to discuss moving into a bigger home—the White House, in Washington, D.C. As he had with his friends and staff, he asked the members of his family for their thoughts on his strengths and weaknesses as a candidate. After some discussion (in which they especially enjoyed discussing his faults!), they agreed he should run.

Hamilton Jordan, Jimmy's executive secretary and chief of staff, managed the campaign. He said Jimmy should keep his intention to run secret for awhile, to give him extra time to prepare before the race got hot.

Preparing for the Presidency

A governor is responsible for knowing about such issues as taxes, water, and education in his state. A President must understand all those matters and much more: defense, energy, and especially foreign affairs.

Jimmy started using his meetings with visitors from other countries to learn more about foreign affairs. During his last two years as governor, he visited 10 countries, including England, Germany, Israel, Brazil, and several countries in Central and South America.

His work on the Trilateral Commission also helped him understand foreign affairs. This group of leaders from Japan, North America, and Europe met every six months to study topics of mutual interest, such as trade, energy, and control of the seas. While a member of the commission, Jimmy met several men he would later bring into his administration: Zbigniew Brzezinski, who became national security advisor; Cyrus R. Vance, who became secretary of state; and Senator Walter F. Mondale, a Democrat from Minnesota who became Jimmy's Vice-President.

Jimmy also changed his reading habits to include books

on foreign affairs, defense, U.S. and world history, and economics – all topics more relevant to running the country. He read biographies of politicians and past Presidents. To avoid making the same mistakes they had, he studied the platforms of every unsuccessful presidential candidate.

The Unknown Candidate

In March 1973, Jimmy was appointed cochairman of the national Democratic Party's 1974 campaign committee. Part of his job was to analyze the issues and personalities in that year's 35 governors' races, 34 campaigns for the U.S. Senate, and 435 elections for the U.S. House of Representatives. It taught him a lot about the men and women all over the country who were trying to be elected to office, the issues they thought were important, and their positions on those issues.

In addition, it was a perfect position from which to travel around the country, meeting people who might support his bid for the presidency without saying that was his purpose. During 1973 and 1974, he met many Democratic leaders and candidates for office, and many leaders of labor, farm, and teaching organizations.

Just as he had been unknown throughout Georgia when he ran for governor, now Jimmy was unknown throughout the nation. In December 1973, he appeared on the television show "What's My Line?" on which three people try to guess a person's identity. None of them knew who Jimmy was, even after they were told he was a governor. Clearly there was much work yet to be done.

In October 1974, Jimmy's staff began to drop hints that he might be a presidential candidate. Then, on December 12, before any other candidate had done so, he made it official.

Chapter 6

"I'll Never Lie to You"

Pesident Lyndon B. Johnson ordered American planes to drop bombs into the steaming jungles of North Vietnam in February 1965, when it looked like South Vietnamese soldiers would not be able to fight off the southward march of the invading communists (Viet Cong) from North Vietnam. In March, 3,500 U.S. Marines landed in South Vietnam. By early 1968, 510,000 American troops were fighting the Viet Cong alongside the South Vietnamese in their civil war halfway around the world. The theory was that if the United States let South Vietnam fall to the Communists, the rest of the countries in Southeast Asia—and who knew where else?—would fall too, like dominoes.

AN UNPOPULAR WAR

In nearly three years of massive bombings that followed, huge regions of both North and South Vietnam were destroyed—but not the enemy's will. Johnson came to see the war as unwinnable. President Richard M. Nixon enlarged the fighting to neighboring Laos and Cambodia in order to destroy Viet Cong bases there.

By 1975, however, most American troops had been withdrawn from South Vietnam. Saigon, South Vietnam's capital, fell in April of that year as the North Vietnamese streamed into the country and took control.

The war that had torn America apart had been lost. More than 58,000 American troops had died, and more than 153,000 had been wounded. Soldiers were spat upon and cursed as they returned home. It was easily the most unpopular war in U.S. history. Students across the country had rioted to stop it; some had even been killed. No one could quite understand what, if anything, America had gained by fighting in South Vietnam. What America had lost, however, was much clearer.

THE WATERGATE AFFAIR

At 2:30 in the morning of June 17, 1972, five men wearing business suits and rubber gloves broke into the Democratic Party's national headquarters in Washington's Watergate Hotel carrying electronic eavesdropping equipment. They worked for the Committee to Re-elect the President, a Republican organization to re-elect Richard Nixon as President in 1972.

In April 1973, President Nixon accepted responsibility for what happened at the Watergate Hotel but repeatedly denied having any knowledge of the event. However, hours of conversation that he had secretly taped in his office at the White House showed that he had, in fact, known about Watergate and had tried to steer the Federal Bureau of Investigation away from investigating the White House.

The President said on national television, "I am not a crook." He was not widely believed, and a congressional committee investigating Watergate voted to impeach (officially accuse) him for obstructing justice. On August 9, 1974, President

Nixon resigned in disgrace, and his Vice-President, Gerald R. Ford, took over.

MAKING PROMISES

In Jimmy Carter's view, Americans were deeply wounded, embarrassed, and discouraged after Vietnam and Watergate. Many felt they had been cheated, lied to, and let down by their government. Therefore, he thought, there was no single issue, like the economy or nuclear weapons, that would guide his campaign. *What* the next President would do mattered – it mattered a great deal – but *who he was* mattered even more. What was most important was repairing the relationship between the President and the people.

"Can our government be honest, decent, open, fair, and compassionate?" he asked, responding to doubts raised by Watergate. "Can our government be competent?" he asked, referring to Vietnam.

The answer to those questions is yes, Jimmy said. "There is a simple and effective way for public officials to regain public trust – *be trustworthy!*" Jimmy wanted to open most secret meetings to the public, control lobbyists, and appoint judges and diplomats strictly on the basis of their qualifications and not as political favors.

It was Carter's belief that government could be competent, efficient, and economical, but first it must be analyzed and then drastically simplified. Every part of government must have clear policies and goals, which he felt were completely lacking.

Jimmy also believed that politicians had underestimated the quality and character of Americans instead of representing their highest ideals. He was firmly convinced that the American people had the strength, character, intelligence, ex-

Carter's presidential campaign headquarters in Plains was a refurbished Seaboard Coastline Railroad depot. (Charles M. Rafshoon.)

perience, patriotism, idealism, compassion, and sense of brotherhood to restore greatness to the country.

In his campaign for President, Jimmy Carter promised a lot. Above all, he promised honesty. "There will be times when I'm asked a question that I might refuse to answer. But if I give an answer, it will be the truth," he said. "If I ever tell a lie, if I ever mislead you, if I ever betray a trust or a confidence, I want you to come and take me out of the White House."

He had a soft southern drawl, piercing blue eyes, and a big, toothy smile that became his trademark. He promised openness, compassion, fairness, sensitivity—and "a government filled with love." He also promised competence, efficiency, and economy. His campaign slogan incorporated his trademark question: "For the American Third Century, Why Not Our Best?"

"Our best" referred to qualities in the people—and to himself.

WHO IS HE?

"Just who is this man to promise all that? Who's heard of him? Where did he come from? Who talks about love in a political campaign? And what's all this talk about being a 'born again' Baptist?"

Those were some of the questions people were asking themselves and each other in the 25 states Jimmy visited within his first few months after leaving the governor's office in January 1975. Here's what he answered: "I am a Southerner, a farmer, an engineer, a businessman, a planner, a scientist, a governor. . . . I am an environmentalist, I am a nuclear physicist, I am an outdoors man, I am a Christian, and I don't see any conflict among these things." Some people worried, though, that there might indeed be conflicts.

A Deeply Religious Person

It is a basic principle of American government that "church and state" must remain separate—that religion must not interfere with government, and vice-versa. People had three big questions: Would Jimmy Carter be able to keep that separation? Was he a fanatic? Would he try to inflict his religion on others? Especially nervous were Jews and Catholics, both minorities in the United States.

Jimmy Carter's Religion

Jimmy Carter is a born-again Southern Baptist. Being "born again" means developing, or suddenly experiencing, a personal relationship with Jesus Christ.

Baptists are the largest group of Protestants in the United States. Protestants, in turn, are the largest religious group in the country, with 78.7 million members, compared to Catholics (52.3 million) and Jews (5.8 million). Baptists baptize (dip in water to symbolize purification) youngsters or adults who believe Jesus Christ is their savior. Jimmy was baptized when he was 11 years old.

The first Baptist leader was John Smyth, who broke off from the English Congregationalists in the early 1600s. Early Baptist churches were founded in Providence, Rhode Island, by Roger Williams in 1638, and later in Philadelphia.

Southern Baptists make up half the Baptists in the United States, with about 13 million members in all 50 states, but they live mostly in the South. About 2,300 Southern Baptist missionaries operate in the United States and in other countries. Southern Baptists split off from other Baptists in 1845 over a quarrel about whether slaveholders should be appointed missionaries. (The Southern Baptists said they should.)

Most U.S. Presidents have been Protestant. Of those, only two—Warren G. Harding (1921–1923) and Harry S. Truman

(1945–1953)—have been Baptist. Only one President, John F. Kennedy (1961–1963), has been Catholic. There have been no Jewish Presidents.

Carter said he could maintain the separation between church and state, and his record showed that he could. As governor, he had opposed laws banning the sale of liquor on Sundays, ended the daily religious services Governor Lester Maddox had held in the capitol, and fought against language in the new Georgia constitution requiring the worship of God. "I don't look on the Presidency as a pastorate [or] look on it with religious connotations," he said.

Though he was obviously very religious, Carter did not seem to be fanatical about it. Occasionally, he even drank and swore! His religious beliefs had "no particular political significance," he said. They are "something that's with me every day." He also did not seem interested in encouraging others to become religious. "If there are those who don't want to vote for me because I'm a deeply committed Christian, I believe they should vote for someone else," he said.

A Southerner and an Outsider

Carter noted that some people discriminate against southerners because of their accent, their culture, their traditional conservatism, and their position in the Civil War. But, he also noted, such discrimination was not only unjust, it was decreasing. He pointed out that when John F. Kennedy, an Irish Catholic liberal, was running for President in 1960, he won in Georgia by a larger percentage than in his home state of Massachusetts. He urged Americans to be that open-minded again.

Many past Presidents had held office in Congress, which made them familiar with how the federal government works. To his regret, Jimmy had not. But rather than apologize for being "an outsider," he claimed it would give him a fresh start, free from entanglement with Congress or with the media (newspapers, television, and radio).

He used his "outsider" status by suggesting to voters that they, too, were outsiders, excluded from power, and that they would become insiders with him. "The time has come for the great majority of Americans—those who have for too long been on the outside looking in—to have a President who will turn the government of this country inside out," he said.

A Man of Many Qualities

Jimmy Carter seemed to have an unusual combination of qualities. He was analytical, using his high intelligence to solve complex problems. And he was stubborn and tough: "I don't let anybody push me around. . . . I wouldn't be a . . . timid President," he said. Yet he was sensitive and compassionate, with a deep concern for the underprivileged and ill.

Although scientifically inclined, Carter enjoyed music and literature and often quoted philosophy. Even his musical tastes were perhaps an unusual combination: he liked classical music, Bob Dylan, Paul Simon, and the Allman Brothers. Despite his obvious gifts, he claimed he was humble. "I am no big shot," he said. "I am not anybody's boss. I want to be everybody's servant."

Jimmy was a liberal with regard to human rights, civil rights, and the environment. Yet he was a conservative in managing government. However, he did not like to call himself by either term.

Presidential candidate Carter receives the endorsement of the Reverend Martin Luther King, Sr., at a rally in Atlanta, Georgia, in 1976. (Charles M. Rafshoon.)

Some people—among them, many reporters—thought Jimmy avoided labeling himself and discussing specific issues so he could appeal to everyone and offend no one, as politicians often do. A different interpretation is that his ability to tolerate ambiguity (lack of clarity) was another of his gifts. "It's difficult to label me, I realize," he said. "But it's equally difficult to narrowly define any individual."

Above all, Carter was enormously self-confident. Because of his religion, he said he felt sure about himself deep inside. Then, again stressing being an outsider, he said, "[Former President] Johnson never felt secure inside, especially around the Eastern establishment—the professors, experts, writers, and media people—and that's why they got him in the end. But I don't feel ill at ease in a Harvard professor's house, or when I'm talking with experts on foreign policy or on economics, or when I'm with the leader of any group."

While campaigning, he said to a little boy, "Hello, Bobby. I'm Jimmy Carter, and I'm going to be your next President. And I'm going to be a wonderful President."

No one had ever met anyone like Jimmy Carter before. As one expert said, he was extraordinary but ordinary. When people did meet him, most of them liked him.

ON THE CAMPAIGN TRAIL

Showing his typical energy, by the end of 1975 Jimmy had visited 43 states and established campaign offices in 17 of them. As had been true in all of his earlier races, his family helped out. If he could not be there to meet voters, Rosalynn, Chip, Caron (Chip's wife), or Lillian's sister would make an appearance. And, as they had always done, the campaigners stayed in supporters' homes whenever possible, to save money and deepen relationships.

Jimmy's objective was to shake the hands of as many Americans as possible. Once, in a Mississippi department store, he reached out to shake the hand of a mannequin. "Better give her a brochure, too," he said to the laughing crowd.

In the symbolically important first Democratic primary election, held in New Hampshire on February 24, 1976, Jimmy won. And, with a few exceptions, he kept on winning all the way through May, when he lost in several states. Out of 30 primaries he entered, he won 18, losing mainly in the

Northeast and the West. When it became clear he was the leader, Jimmy chose Walter Mondale as his vice-presidential running mate.

It had been a long climb up from anonymity. Jimmy accepted the Democratic nomination at the party's convention in New York City on June 15, 1976. He opened his acceptance speech by joking, "My name is Jimmy Carter, and I'm running for President."

Up Against Ford

Moving his headquarters from Plains to Atlanta, Jimmy entered the campaign's second half: doing battle against President Gerald R. Ford, the incumbent. One month after the Democratic convention, public opinion polls showed Jimmy leading Ford by 33 percentage points. But during the campaign, Ford gained strength.

Some of Ford's gains were caused by Jimmy's mistakes. In a September interview with *Playboy* magazine, Jimmy admitted that he had "looked on a lot of women with lust" and "committed adultery in [his] heart many times." He went on to make a good point—that God forgave such thoughts but not the actions they led to—but attention focused on his admission. Earlier he had said, "Watch me closely during the campaign, because I won't be any better a President than I am a candidate." The *Playboy* incident made people wonder about his judgment and shook their confidence in him as "a good Christian." It gave Ford ammunition to attack Jimmy, and he used it.

In the first of three televised debates against Ford, the polls said Jimmy lost. In the second, Ford incorrectly said Russia did not dominate Yugoslavia, Rumania, Poland, and other Eastern European countries, and Jimmy won big. The third debate's winner was unclear.

In his speeches, Jimmy continued to attack "the insiders" in Washington. For awhile, each candidate attacked the other's character. Ford called Jimmy "a man who will say anything, anywhere to be President." Jimmy, in turn, sarcastically called Ford a leader "in the great tradition of Warren Harding, Herbert Hoover, and Richard Nixon."

By election day, November 2, 1976, Ford was leading in the polls by one point. It was not until 3:30 in the morning that Jimmy was declared the winner. It had been close — not what Jimmy had hoped for. He won only 50.1 percent of the popular vote, compared to Ford's 48 percent, and only 297 electoral delegates to Ford's 240. But he was President.

Chapter 7

A Very Short Honeymoon

January 20, 1977, was bitterly cold. Still, thousands of people lined the mall that stretches over a mile from the U.S. Capitol to the White House as President Jimmy Carter and his family started up the parade route. Suddenly, the President's motorcade stopped. He, Rosalynn, and their children climbed out of their cars. The crowd murmured, afraid of what might be wrong.

With their family, Jimmy and Rosalynn joined hands and started walking. A shock wave went through the crowd. "They're walking! They're walking!" people cried. Some of them wept openly. When Jimmy saw them, a few tears of joy ran down his own cold cheeks.

A POPULIST PRESIDENT

The inauguration day walk was only the first of many symbols Jimmy Carter used to continue his effort at showing he was a populist—a common man, a man of the people. He was sworn in as "Jimmy Carter," not his full name, and wore an old suit at the ceremony. At the 11 parties held that evening, Rosalynn wore the same dress she had worn when Jimmy was inaugurated as governor.

Newly inaugurated President Jimmy Carter and his wife, Rosalynn, wave to the cheering crowd as they walk the 1.2 miles of the inauguration day parade route on January 20, 1977. (Jimmy Carter Library.)

Jimmy cut back the number of cars and drivers available to his staff and enrolled Amy, then 9, in a mostly black public school near the White House. He sold the presidential yacht *Sequoia,* and he carried his own garment bag when flying.

Some people said Jimmy had gone too far. They liked their President to live differently than they did. To appease them, Jimmy restored the traditional playing of "Hail to the Chief" on special occasions, but that was about all the presidential privileges he did restore.

Settling In and Picking a Team

As the new occupants of the White House, Jimmy and Rosalynn were entitled to redecorate it in any way they wanted. Instead, they left it much as it was, valuing the historic furnishings. In the Cabinet Room, where he met with his most trusted advisors, Jimmy did hang portraits of the Presidents he most admired: Thomas Jefferson, Abraham Lincoln, and Harry Truman. He chose warm colors and fabrics for his study, a small room near the Oval Office. One of his most prized possessions, a large globe, stood within arm's reach of his leather swivel chair.

Jimmy established a routine of getting to the Oval Office by 6:30 every morning. He started each day with coffee, two newspapers, and an overnight report on the state of the world. On cold days he made a fire. Appointments and meetings began at 8:00 A.M. He met Rosalynn once a week to talk business over lunch.

Back in December, Jimmy (always with Rosalynn's help) had chosen some of the many people who would help him do his job. He picked his old acquaintance, Hamilton Jordan, as his chief aide. Jody Powell became his press secretary. Among his top advisors, some of the most important or controversial were Zbigniew Brzezinski, national security advisor; Cyrus Vance, secretary of state; T. Bertram ("Bert") Lance, director of the Office of Management and Budget (OMB); and Andrew Young, ambassador to the United Nations. Jordan, Powell, and Brzezinski could stop by Jimmy's office without appointments. He preferred others to phone ahead.

Despite his many advisors, in his early days—and later—Jimmy felt lonely making the many important decisions a President must make. He prayed often for a clear mind and sound judgment.

At first Jimmy was overwhelmed by the 60 or 70 documents he had to read every day. He was taking work home every night instead of spending evenings as he wanted: reading, seeing a movie, or just being with his family. By having assistants deal with some of the work, telling people to write shorter memos, and taking another speed-reading course, he was able to reduce the load.

Working With Congress

All Presidents are given a "honeymoon" when they start their term: several months when the press, the people, and Congress are gentle and supportive. A good relationship between the President and Congress—100 senators and 435 representatives, all of whom are part of the Washington "mess" Jimmy had criticized relentlessly while campaigning—is essential to the President's success. Jimmy joked that his honeymoon with Congress lasted a week. There was some truth to his joke.

After only a short time in office, Jimmy angered many legislators by blocking, as wasteful and unnecessary, the dams, lakes, canals, and many other projects they had promised their constituents. Then he asked the same legislators to vote for projects that he supported but that were opposed by strong special-interest groups upon whom they depended for financial support. One senator complained to him, "Mr. President, if I vote 'right' many more times, I'm going to lose the next election!"

Jimmy wasted no time pushing for the laws he most wanted passed: an energy policy and permission to reorganize the government.

"THE MORAL EQUIVALENT OF WAR"

The United States depended on a few Latin American and Middle Eastern countries for much of its oil. That meant those oil-producing countries, several of which had joined together to form OPEC (the Organization of Petroleum Exporting Countries), had a powerful influence over America. We were "being jerked around by a few desert states," Jimmy said. Because many other countries also depended on OPEC for oil, prices were high and supplies were limited. Jimmy wanted to cut back on energy use, control domestic oil and natural gas prices, and encourage the use of alternative fuels, such as solar energy.

The People Resist

During the winter of 1977 petroleum supplies fell so low that many states suffered a gasoline shortage. And many schools and factories dependent on oil for heating had to close. Jimmy thought the problem was such an emergency that he said he would create an energy plan within three months and wanted Congress to enact it in his first year as President.

But Jimmy found that Americans were reluctant to turn down the heat in their homes, join car pools, or make other sacrifices to save fuel. Many people thought gas and oil companies were just faking the shortage to make more money.

In February, Jimmy appeared on a televised "fireside chat" wearing a heavy cardigan sweater rather than a suit, both to seem an "ordinary guy" and to emphasize the need to save energy by turning down the heat. On April 18, he went on television again, this time to declare "the moral equivalent of war" on energy waste and imported oil. Two days later, he presented to Congress his complex program to ease the crisis, seeking both greater conservation and greater production. *Time* magazine called it "the most intensive effort by a U.S. President, in or out of wartime, to rally the nation behind a common cause."

Enacting Phase 1

Congress was slow to act, however, because the representatives of so many powerful interest groups wanted to have a say in the new energy laws. These groups included producers and users of oil, gas, coal, and nuclear energy; automobile manufacturers; and environmentalists. Finally, on August 4, the Department of Energy was created to pull together more than 50 different federal agencies and thus better coordinate the nation's energy policy. But by year's end, Congress still had not enacted Jimmy's program, mostly because of heavy lobbying by the energy industries.

A "bitter struggle" with Congress to address the country's energy problems would occupy Jimmy until the end of his term. This issue was his most important domestic goal. He blamed Congress for the delay in enacting his energy program; legislators, in turn, accused him of hostility and insensitivity to the legislative process.

In July 1978, when Jimmy attended an international conference on energy, he was embarrassed that the United States still had not resolved its energy problems. It had been over a year since he had presented his energy program to Congress.

Finally, in October 1978 Congress approved all five pieces of legislation making up the first phase of Jimmy's energy package. Under the new laws, car manufacturers would be fined for producing "gas guzzlers"; the use of coal, solar heating, and car pools would be rewarded; and more efficient home appliances would be required. Jimmy had even more ideas for reducing energy use, holding down its price, and creating alternative sources of energy. But these ideas would have to wait until the next year's congressional session.

The Camp David "Summit"

In January and February 1979, a revolution in Iran nearly stopped oil production there, causing a worldwide oil shortage. Automobile drivers had to line up for gas, first in California and then everywhere in the country. Gas was rationed, and signs saying "Sorry, No Gas" became increasingly common. On April 5, Jimmy addressed the nation again to propose more energy conservation measures. By July, the fuel shortage had become acute in the Northeast and East.

A poll in May showed most Americans thought the "shortage" was a fraud by the oil companies to raise prices. Only a third of the people polled believed American energy demands were excessive.

On July 3 Jimmy went to Camp David, a 143-acre presidential retreat in the Catoctin Mountains in Maryland, to prepare yet another televised address to the nation on energy. However, less than 24 hours before airtime, he cancelled the speech. His calls for conservation were being ignored, and Congress was not cooperating. Something drastic had to be done.

From July 6 through July 16, Jimmy invited 134 guests to Camp David to advise him on why people were not listening to him and why his leadership seemed to be failing. During many long meetings, the guests discussed each member of Jimmy's Cabinet and staff. And they discussed *him*, more critically than anyone else. Even then, Jimmy took careful notes. Most guests acknowledged his intelligence and ability to solve problems but doubted his capacity to act effectively, based mainly on the long struggle he was having with Congress over the energy crisis.

"A Crisis of Confidence"

On July 15, Jimmy appeared on television to tell what he had learned at Camp David. He said Americans were suffering a "crisis of confidence" in their government. Restoring faith would require a collective sacrifice for the public good: carpools, fewer car trips, more use of public transportation, and lowered thermostats.

Jimmy then explained the further details of his energy program. It would tax part of the profits of American oil companies and require the companies to put another part of their profits into increased exploration and production. The program would also remove government controls from oil prices and encourage the development of synthetic fuels.

Jimmy called the speech "a warning in harsh terms, terms not often used by a President speaking to the people of our country."

Two days after the speech, acting on recommendations he had received at Camp David, Jimmy asked for the resignations of all 13 members of his Cabinet. He accepted four of them. Jimmy intended the shake-up as a gesture of strength and determination to strengthen his staff, but it was widely seen as a governmental crisis. Even he later admitted the changes were handled "very poorly."

Success At Last

The last part of Jimmy's energy package became law in the spring of 1980. It created a company to manufacture synthetic fuels and passed the largest tax ever imposed on an industry, taking $227 billion from the oil companies over a 13-year period.

The fight had been "bruising," but it had succeeded. Americans were importing and using less oil, and oil prices had dropped. Jimmy had no doubt America would now be better able to handle whatever energy problems the future might bring.

REORGANIZATION AND MORE

Jimmy Carter put more legislative proposals before Congress during his first six months in office than had any President since Franklin D. Roosevelt in 1933. Besides energy, another of his important domestic goals as President was to reorganize the federal government in much the same way he had reorganized the state government in Georgia. He wanted to pass a law that would automatically put into effect any reorganization plans he gave to Congress if Congress did not reject them. (The usual pattern is that proposals automatically die unless Congress acts on them.) Thanks to help from some Republicans, his reorganization bill was passed on March 31, 1980.

The issue of whether to build a fleet of B-1 bombers was a problem previous Presidents and Congresses had not been able to solve. Powerful military and industrial lobbies supported the sleek new plane. But each one cost $100 million to produce, and Jimmy thought the planes were ineffective and "a gross waste of money." He favored unmanned missiles, which are accurate, harder to intercept, and 100 times less expensive. On June 30, despite strong pressure, he announced the B-1 bomber would not be built.

Also during 1980, the airline industry was deregulated (made more competitive, in theory, by removal of government controls), and the mandatory retirement age was raised from 65 to 70.

Jimmy blamed Congress and lobbyists—"powerful and ravenous wolves"—for the defeat of his proposed welfare reform, tax reform, and national health care programs. But despite the friction between Jimmy and Congress, he was able to enact 75.4 percent of his first year's proposals. In comparison, Kennedy had scored 81 percent in his first year; Johnson had scored 88 percent.

Lance in Trouble

"We were somewhat ostentatious about setting a high moral standard for ourselves, and so my administration was not to be given any room for error by the press," Jimmy noted regretfully. "It is impossible to overestimate the damage inflicted on my administration by charges leveled against Bert Lance."

A very close friend and confidante of Jimmy's, Lance was the first person he invited into his administration. To serve as budget director, Lance, like all appointees, had to reveal his finances and remove any possible conflicts of interest. He promised to sell his stocks in several Georgia banks he had headed, but it turned out that doing so would cost him, the banks, and the banks' other shareholders a great deal of money.

In early July 1977, at Jimmy's request, a Senate committee considered allowing Lance to hold on to his bank stocks temporarily. In the course of its consideration, the committee raised serious questions about the legality of Lance's conduct as a banker. Investigations by both Houses of Congress and six federal agencies during the next three months continually revealed new evidence that Lance had allowed overdrafts (checks without money behind them) by his wife's family, made loans without adequate collateral (security), and generally disregarded banking laws.

Jimmy saw the affair as a creation of the media, "an investigative reporter's dream." Though he knew it was damaging his reputation, he stood firmly behind Lance until September 21, 1977, when he accepted Lance's resignation.

Lance was indicted for obtaining loans for personal benefit but was never convicted. Jimmy did not regret having defended Lance, but he did learn a lesson: to associate with people who even appear to act improperly is risky when you claim higher standards of behavior.

The Embarrassing Ambassador

A black congressman from Georgia and one of Carter's earliest, strongest supporters in his presidential race, Andrew Young was Jimmy's choice for U.S. ambassador to the United Nations. Before long, though, he became an embarrassment.

In May 1977 Young told reporters that the "old colonial mentality" was still strong in Great Britain and that the Russians and Swedes are racists. In July 1978 he said there were hundreds, perhaps thousands, of political prisoners in America.

Worst of all, on August 13, 1979, Young met with a representative of the Palestine Liberation Organization (PLO), a group sworn to destroy Israel, America's close ally. The United States had pledged never to deal with the PLO until it changed its position. Two days later, Young resigned.

THE ECONOMY

Managing the economy is a major part of a President's job. Two numbers tell a lot about a country's economic health: inflation and unemployment. Inflation measures the decrease in how much a dollar will buy: the higher inflation is, the less money is worth. High inflation can wipe out people's life savings and destroy businesses. Unemployment reveals how many people are out of work.

When Jimmy took office, the inflation rate was 7.2 percent and the unemployment rate was 8.1 percent. By the middle of Jimmy's second year in office, inflation had climbed to 10.8 percent. Not only was that a big increase, it was symbolic, crossing into dangerous "double-digit" inflation.

Unemployment, however, had dropped to 5.7 percent, in part because of job programs Jimmy built that would create 10 million jobs by the end of his term. But polls showed most Americans cared more about inflation than unemployment.

At the end of 1979, unemployment stood at 6 percent but inflation had climbed to 13.3 percent. It now took $223.70 to buy what would have cost $100 in 1967. It was the worst inflation since 1953, and nearly twice the 7.2 percent rate Jimmy had inherited from President Ford.

In early 1980, inflation was running at a terrifying 20 percent, mostly because of OPEC's increases in oil prices. During the spring, the country went into a brief but steep recession (economic downturn). Inflation dropped rapidly to around 7 percent by October 1980.

Chapter 8

"No More War, No More Bloodshed"

O n May 14, 1948, the state of Israel was born. Already home to about 1.26 million Arabs, the new state contained about 678,000 Jews, many of whom had fled the Nazi Holocaust, which killed six million Jews throughout Europe. For the first time since 70 A.D., the Jews ruled their own homeland.

That same day, the Egyptian Army invaded Israel across its southern border. Over the next 25 years, Israel and its Arab neighbors would fight four major wars. Egypt would be a principal aggressor in all the attempts to "drive the Jews into the sea."

On March 26, 1979, Egyptian President Anwar el-Sadat, Israeli Prime Minister Menachem Begin, and U.S. President Jimmy Carter clasped hands and beamed, with each nation's flag in the background. After months of preliminary visits and an intense 13-day bargaining session, the two ancient enemies sat at the same table and signed a treaty that they hoped would bring peace to their countries. Watching on the White House lawn, 1,600 guests cheered the seemingly impossible moment.

For years afterwards, an Israeli radio station, the Voice of Peace, would use as station identification the recorded words Sadat spoke so movingly: "No more war, no more bloodshed."

WORKING FOR PEACE

When President Carter took office in 1977, Egypt was officially at war with Israel. Egypt was also participating in an Arab boycott of Israel and had closed the Suez Canal to Israeli ships. Like all Arab leaders, Sadat officially refused to admit Israel was a state or even had a right to exist. Frequent terrorist killings, problems with refugees, and refusals to negotiate dimmed hopes for peace.

The relationship between Israel and the United States had always been close. Americans felt warmly toward the tiny democracy and gave it money, arms, and support. But President Carter felt that continued tension between Israel and its neighbors could be a threat to U.S. interests in the region. Though his advisors warned him not to get involved with the Middle East, he was confident he could help bring peace to the area.

When Carter first met Sadat, on April 4, 1977, in Washington, he found an "easy and natural friendship" between them. He was impressed by Sadat, a Moslem so devout he had a callus on his forehead from touching the ground when bowing toward the holy city of Mecca. Of all the Arab heads of state Jimmy met that first year, Sadat was the only one who publicly said he would deal with Israel. All of them, including Sadat, were scared of being killed for even agreeing to talk about peace with Israel.

Sadat in Israel

Despite a number of meetings between Carter and Israeli and Arab leaders, no progress was made until November 1977, when, through Jimmy, Sadat asked Begin to invite him to Israel. Much of the world was thrilled when, on November 19,

Sadat arrived in Jerusalem to address the Israeli Knesset (parliament). Sadat had taken a huge risk. Syria broke off relations with Egypt, and officials in Syria, Libya, and Iraq called for Sadat's assassination.

Despite frequent meetings after that between Jimmy, Sadat, Begin, and other Israeli leaders, the good feelings from Sadat's visit to Jerusalem led to no real progress in 1977. Begin and Sadat never spoke to each other directly, and once Sadat even publicly discussed going to war. Again, Jimmy's advisors suggested he avoid becoming involved in Mideast negotiations because it would be "a losing proposition." But he felt he could not abandon the attempt, so he invited Begin and Sadat to spend some time talking together at Camp David.

THE CAMP DAVID CONFERENCE

To prepare for this historic occasion, Carter studied psychological profiles of the two heads of state and spent hours planning his strategy. He ordered the meetings closed to the press so Begin and Sadat would not feel pressure to come up with quick results.

On September 5, 1978, Sadat and Begin joined Carter at Camp David. As the talks began, Jimmy met with each leader separately, noting their differences. Begin was formal, always wearing a coat and tie, while Sadat wore sports clothes. Begin would join the Americans, Israelis, and Egyptians for meals, while Sadat preferred to eat alone in his cabin. Begin was ready to work night or day; Sadat kept a tight schedule of work, exercise, diet, and sleep.

Feelings between Begin and Sadat were unfriendly, and the two were far apart on nearly every issue, including the purpose of their being there. Begin thought the talks would produce only general agreements, which would form a basis for future meetings where the specifics could be resolved.

Sadat wanted to create a firm framework for peace right then and there.

Sadat put his complete trust in Jimmy, revealing what his negotiating positions on the issues would be and, in contrast, what he would really accept at the end of the bargaining. The Israelis never revealed that information.

Sadat demanded, among other things, that Egypt must get back all the land Israel had conquered during its wars with the Arabs. Begin insisted Israel would never return the air bases and 13 settlements (populated by 2,000 Israelis) it had built in the Sinai Desert after capturing it from Egypt during the 1967 war.

Despite the differences between them, both Sadat and Begin thought of themselves as strong men of destiny who held the fate of their nations in their hands. And neither they nor Carter wanted to fail in front of the world.

Sitting Down Together

Carter, Begin, and Sadat met together for the first time in the afternoon of the first day at Camp David. Sadat read a proposal that was extremely harsh, blaming all the wars on Israel and requiring Israel to give up East Jerusalem and allow a Palestinian nation to be formed in Israeli territory. Jimmy could feel Begin's tension building. When Sadat finished, no one spoke for a moment. Then Jimmy suggested that if Begin would just sign the proposal, it would save everybody a lot of time. All three of them broke into hilarious laughter, and the tension eased.

The next day, Jimmy quietly took notes, without looking up, forcing the two old enemies to start talking directly to each other and not through him. But the discussion soon broke down into a long, heated argument, with only occasional periods of calm. Jimmy acted as a referee, repeatedly guiding the discussion back onto track. After three hours,

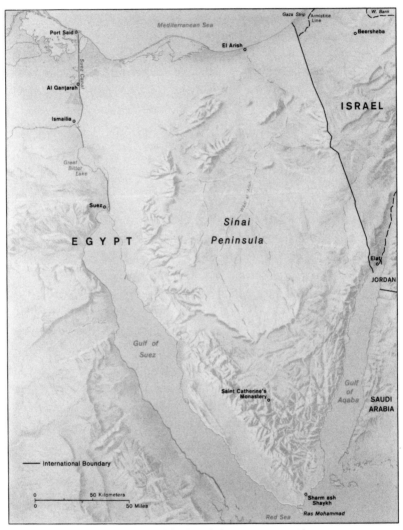

The Sinai Peninsula was captured by Israel during its war with Egypt in 1967. The land was later returned to Egypt under the terms of the Camp David agreements. (Library of Congress.)

however, Sadat and Begin had done little except to identify the difficult issues.

That afternoon, the two leaders began arguing again. After awhile, they stood up, not looking at each other, and edged toward the door. But Jimmy blocked their exit, urging them to give him another chance and to have confidence in him. Begin and Sadat then left without speaking to each other. It was the last time they would meet face to face at Camp David.

Shuttle Diplomacy

For the rest of the 11 days the three men spent at Camp David, Jimmy shuttled back and forth between Sadat and Begin, presenting each with the other's proposals and reactions. The main problem continued to be the Sinai settlements.

In private meetings with Jimmy, Begin spent hours arguing fiercely over details, like the meaning of important words: "autonomy," "Palestinian," "withdrawal." Sadat was more concerned with broad policy.

During the long, tense days, Jimmy and the American team prepared 23 versions of the peace "framework," a general outline for peace. Carter himself wrote eight of them. Progress was terribly slow and difficult.

Frustrated beyond endurance, Sadat came to Carter on the eighth day to say he was leaving. Jimmy reminded him that the Egyptians had five divisions of soldiers lined up to fight Israel. A peace treaty between Egypt and Israel would free up those troops and make them available against his potential enemies in Libya and Ethiopia. Sadat was impressed with Carter's argument and went back to his cabin.

Despite continued hard work by all three men and their teams, on the 11th day Jimmy began to feel there was no hope. Nevertheless, he was shocked when an aide burst into his room and told Carter that Sadat and his party were packed and awaiting the arrival of a helicopter. Jimmy took Sadat aside into his cabin. He told Sadat that if he left he would be breaking a personal promise, hurting the relationship between the United States and Egypt, wrecking the talks, and ruining his reputation as a peacemaker. Again, Sadat changed his mind.

An Embrace for Success

Though discouraged, Jimmy still did not want to give up. Finally, on the 13th day, Begin, with cries of "excessive demands" and "political suicide," agreed to ask the Knesset to vote on whether to evict the Sinai settlers. The three leaders embraced. It was 10 at night on September 17, 1978, when they arrived at the White House to sign the framework agreements and announce their success to the world.

For the first time, it looked like there could be peace between Israel and Egypt, due directly to the skill, determination, and courage of Jimmy Carter. But none of the three leaders knew how far they still had to go.

Working Out the Details

Carter wanted to extend the new peace agreement between Israel and Egypt to other Arab countries. He sent Secretary of State Vance to Jordan, Saudi Arabia, and Syria to meet their leaders and tell them what had happened at Camp David. But none of those leaders wanted to join in the agreement unless Yassir Arafat, leader of the Palestine Liberation Organization, would do so, and he refused.

Later the Knesset voted to approve the framework agreements and remove the Israeli settlers from the Sinai desert. It was, as Jimmy said, "a remarkable demonstration of political courage on the part of Prime Minister Begin, who had to go against his own previous commitments over a lifetime

With their countries' flags as a backdrop, Anwar Sadat (left), Jimmy Carter, and Menachem Begin clasp hands after the signing of the Camp David agreements on September 17, 1978. (Jimmy Carter Library.)

and against his own closest friends." Begin's car was splat-tered with eggs and tomatoes, and a militant Israeli climbed onto it and broke the windshield.

Sadat, too, was under pressure. Other Arab countries did not want Egypt to make peace without them, and they did not want to make peace at all.

Fights over details still threatened to derail the agree-ment. Begin, in particular, was difficult and negative, mak-ing it necessary for Carter to continue writing versions of a treaty with terms that were just a little less than what each side wanted. In despair, he finally decided to visit Israel and Egypt for a last attempt at reaching peace. If it failed, the trip would seem an expensive waste, so Jimmy was taking another chance.

When he arrived in Israel, Carter asked Begin if he really wanted a peace treaty, because Begin appeared to be doing everything he could do to obstruct it. But when Jimmy and Begin visited Yad Vashem, the Holocaust memorial, it be-came much easier for Jimmy to understand Begin's extreme caution.

Carter was shocked at the shouting, interruptions, and rudeness that Begin had to face when speaking in the Knesset. But Begin seemed to relish the combat, proud of the display of democracy at work. The details were worked out.

After the treaty was signed in March 1979, Sadat and Begin tried to outdo each other in making peace. Sadat said that together, he and Begin would take from Jimmy the bur-den of further negotiations. "If you do, my fervent prayers will have been answered," Jimmy said.

Chapter 9
Foreign Tensions

D uring his administration, President Carter had important dealings with four countries – China, the Soviet Union, Panama, and Iran – on the subjects of human rights violations, nuclear weapons, or political stability.

In addition, some minor disputes over human rights violations involved the countries of Argentina, Ethiopia, and Uruguay. Carter directed that money being sent by the United States to those countries be cut off. Evidence had surfaced regarding torture of political prisoners as well as other violations. The Carter administration also targeted the country of Brazil as violating human rights. The Brazilian government was so offended by these accusations that it refused to accept any further American aid.

THE SOVIET UNION AND HUMAN RIGHTS

Expanding human rights – not just the freedom from torture but the rights to emigrate; to have food, clothing, shelter, medical care, and employment; and to be free from discrimination – was a principal goal of the Carter administration. So was eliminating nuclear weapons from the world.

The two goals clashed in America's relationship with the Soviet Union. The Strategic Arms Limitation Talks (SALT) to reduce the number and power of atomic weapons had been going on between the United States and Russia since November 1969. A limited agreement, known as SALT I, was signed in May 1972, after which the two countries started at once to work on a more complete agreement, SALT II. But Carter felt that too often the United States had been ignoring Russian violations of human rights so as not to jeopardize the arms talks.

In 1977 the Americans had more nuclear warheads with greater accuracy than the Soviets, but the Soviets had more launchers with more total power. Jimmy sent Secretary of State Vance to the Soviet Union in March to open the SALT II talks with a proposal that the armament cuts be much deeper than the United States had ever requested before.

Soviet General Secretary Leonid Brezhnev rejected Carter's proposal. He also angrily objected to Jimmy's having written a letter of support to Andrei D. Sakharov, a distinguished Soviet physicist who was not allowed to leave Russia. Despite resistance from the State Department, which felt he was pushing the Soviets too hard, Jimmy pledged his continued efforts to free Sakharov and expand human rights in Russia. The talks between Vance and Brezhnev lasted only two days.

In May, Vance and Soviet Foreign Minister Andrei Gromyko agreed in Geneva, Switzerland, to resume SALT II, discussing cuts that were not as deep as those Jimmy had proposed earlier. Then, during a meeting between Carter and Gromyko in September 1977, the two countries came to a basic understanding that could form the basis for a treaty.

Speaking Out

On July 5, 1978, the Soviet Union put dissident Anatoly Sharansky on trial as a spy for the U.S. Central Intelligence Agency (CIA). In fact, his only "crimes" were being Jewish and wanting to leave Russia. The year before, Jimmy had declared Sharansky was never a CIA spy—a significant help to Sharansky, because American Presidents rarely comment on such matters. Going further, Jimmy wrote a letter to Brezhnev objecting to the trial and threatened that it could endanger relations between the two countries.

An Unpleasant Visit

Despite the threat, negotiations toward a SALT treaty wore on. Months passed as Carter, Vance, and Gromyko haggled over apparently simple definitions like "new missile," "cruise missile," and "range."

Then, a number of senators visited the Soviet Union over Christmas 1977. They found that the Soviet leaders were heavy-handed, rude, and argumentative hosts. Under the Constitution, two-thirds of the Senate (66 senators) have to ratify treaties before they become law. The Christmas visit made the senators less likely to ratify any treaty the negotiations might produce—not more likely, as Carter had hoped.

President Carter stressed that if the senators refused to ratify a treaty, the number and size of nuclear weapons would simply continue to grow, endangering the entire world. "It is precisely *because* we have fundamental differences with the Soviet Union that we are determined to bring this dangerous dimension of our military competition under control," he said.

Scolding Brezhnev

Carter and a number of his colleagues flew to Vienna on June 15, 1979, for his first meeting with Soviet President Leonid Brezhnev. When they arrived, Secretary of State Vance met with Foreign Minister Gromyko and read him 12 points essential to the SALT agreement. Gromyko rejected each one of them. Jimmy had been advised, though, that the Soviets would make compromises as late as possible, and then only through Brezhnev.

Carter then paid a formal call on Brezhnev at the President of Austria's palace. Brezhnev was frail and in poor health. The air between them was strained. But on the way out the door after an awkward chat, Brezhnev put his hand on Jimmy's shoulder and said, "If we do not succeed, God will not forgive us." As they walked down a few steps, he kept his hand there. Jimmy felt that those gestures bridged the gap between them better than any official talk could have.

The next day, Jimmy quoted Brezhnev's words back to him, subtly using them to pressure Brezhnev. He openly scolded the Russians for making trouble in the Caribbean (especially Cuba), Africa (Angola and Ethiopia), the Middle East (Syria and Iran), and Southeast Asia (Vietnam and Cambodia). But he also promised them that the normalization of relations between the United States and China would never work against the Soviet Union. (The Soviets and the Chinese feared each other, and the Soviets felt more threatened the closer U.S.–China relations became.)

Carter praised the Soviets for having recently increased emigration and said, "Now you need to continue this policy and release Mr. Sharansky and other dissidents." He reminded them he would continue to press for progress on this issue.

Signing the SALT II Treaty

At a ceremony on June 18, 1979, Carter and Brezhnev signed a treaty, binding until January 1985, that limited the number of bombers and missile launchers each side could have. SALT II was "the most detailed, far-reaching, comprehensive treaty in the history of arms control," Jimmy said. He shook hands

Jimmy Carter and Soviet President Leonid Brezhnev sign the SALT II agreements in Vienna, Austria, on June 18, 1979. (Jimmy Carter Library.)

with Brezhnev and, to his surprise, Brezhnev embraced him warmly in Soviet fashion.

Jimmy then mounted an intensive effort to persuade the U.S. Senate to ratify the new treaty. He and other treaty supporters made numerous speeches and held interviews and private briefings to reassure the senators that making peace with Russia did not mean weakening America.

But somehow secret information leaked out that Soviet troops were stationed in Cuba, alarming some senators and the nation generally. To the American government's embarrassment, it turned out that the Soviet troops had been in Cuba for years. The storm died down, and the Senate scheduled debate on the treaty for early in 1980.

The Invasion of Afghanistan

Then, on December 29, 1979, 30,000 Soviet troops invaded Afghanistan. To protest the invasion, on January 4, 1980, Carter stopped the sale of grain and high-technology items (such as computers) to Russia. He also eliminated cultural exchange programs. On April 22, the decision was made not to send an American team to the summer Olympics in Moscow. Eventually, 55 other nations joined the boycott.

Of course, the Soviet invasion of Afghanistan destroyed the already weak congressional support for the SALT treaty. Further efforts to persuade the Senate to ratify it would have been useless. Although both the United States and the Soviet Union agreed to honor the agreement in general, Jimmy called this "the most profound disappointment of my Presidency."

RELATIONS WITH CHINA

China had intrigued Jimmy ever since he was a young boy. He heard stories of Baptist missionaries going to that exotic country to set up schools and hospitals. And an uncle in the Navy sent him photos and letters describing the cities of Shanghai and Tsingtao.

As a submarine officer, Jimmy had visited China, where he bought silk and carvings of ivory and wood. The ports he had called on were occupied at that time by the Nationalist forces of Chiang Kai-shek. However, they were under siege by the troops of Communist leader Mao Tse-tung, whose campfires Jimmy could see burning in the hills.

In October 1949, Mao's troops defeated those of Chiang Kai-shek. Chiang and his followers were forced off the mainland onto the island of Taiwan. American loyalties were with Chiang, and the United States continued to recognize the Nationalists on Taiwan as China's only government. The United States also signed a mutual defense treaty with the Nationalists and stationed troops on the island. But as the years passed, it became obvious Chiang would never be able to retake mainland China. With one billion people — nearly a fourth of the world's population — the People's Republic of China could no longer be ignored.

Though the relationship between China and the Soviet Union had once been close, in 1969 troops from the two countries fought along their common border. The Chinese then started seeking closer ties with the United States to help protect themselves against the Soviets.

Proceeding with Caution

In 1972 President Richard Nixon went to China. In a historic breakthrough, he and Premier Chou En-lai signed a document in Shanghai declaring there was only one China. (By doing so, the United States was saying it would break relations with Taiwan.) But after 1972, feelings between the United States and China became worse, not better. Frightened by the SALT talks between the United States and Russia, the Chinese accused the United States of not being able to make up its mind about friendship with them.

Carter wanted to achieve full diplomatic relations with China — but without betraying Taiwan or straining the U.S. relationship with the Soviet Union. He sent Secretary of State Vance to Peking on August 22, 1977, to talk with Vice-Chairman Deng Xiaoping and Premier Hua Kuofeng. The Chinese continued to insist that before they could proceed with any negotiations, the United States had to break its defense treaty and diplomatic ties with Taiwan and withdraw its military forces from the island country.

Before being elected President, Carter had asked former Secretary of State Henry Kissinger, who had helped negotiate the Shanghai agreement during Nixon's administration, to come to Plains and brief him on China. He learned that the Chinese were tough, clever, patient bargainers. After Vance's fruitless visit to Peking, Carter resolved to present each proposal separately and slowly in order to build up trust among the negotiators. It would take time, but he would be patient.

Normalizing Relations

In May 1978 Carter sent National Security Advisor Brzezinski to Peking to discuss as many issues as possible, but not necessarily to reach an agreement. Through him, Jimmy told the Chinese that "the U.S. has made up its mind."

Relations between the two countries warmed up that summer. Leonard Woodcock, chief of the U.S. liaison office in Peking, began holding talks in secret so as not to arouse opposition from Taiwan supporters. Jimmy personally wrote each carefully worded proposal that Woodcock put forward.

On December 15, 1978, Carter announced that U.S. relations with China would be normalized effective January 1, 1979. That meant the United States and China would exchange ambassadors, buy more of each other's products, and exchange students and cultural programs.

The serious opposition President Carter had anticipated from Congress never came. Even the Taiwanese were not too upset, because the agreement said the United States would maintain its commercial, cultural, and trade relations with Taiwan. In celebration of the agreement, Deng Xiaoping accepted Jimmy's invitation to make his first visit to America early in 1979.

Deng Comes to America

Chinese leader Deng Xiaoping's visit to America in late January 1979 was, as Jimmy put it, "one of the delightful experiences" of his presidency. Carter found Deng "tough, intelligent, frank, courageous, personable, self-assured, and friendly." Jimmy invited former Presidents Nixon and Ford to the White House to attend a cheerful, festive banquet, because each had been part of the efforts toward normalization.

At Washington's Kennedy Center, Deng went up on stage to put his arms around some American children who had sung Chinese songs in his honor. One senator who had opposed normalization said there was no way to stop it in the face of such good feelings.

But in February 1979, Chinese troops crossed into Vietnam. To protest that military action and because they thought normalization betrayed Taiwan, some members of Congress opposed laws that would help establish normal relations with China. Nevertheless, the laws were passed in March. The experience as a whole taught Jimmy "why some people say the Chinese are the most civilized people in the world."

DOING "THE RIGHT THING" IN PANAMA

In 1903, the newly formed Republic of Panama, in Central America, signed a treaty with the United States allowing construction of a canal connecting the Atlantic and Pacific oceans, thereby greatly improving worldwide shipping. The treaty, which was signed by Panama only under threats that the United States would withdraw its military protection if Panama

*Jimmy and Rosalynn admire a gift given to them by Chinese
Vice-Chairman Deng Xiaoping (in right foreground) on January 29, 1979.* (Jimmy Carter Library.)

did not sign, cut the new country in two. America acquired
almost complete control of the 10-mile-wide zone through
which the canal would pass. The canal, 40.3 miles long, was
completed in 1914.

Riots broke out in 1964 in Panama over who controlled
the Canal Zone. Four American soldiers and 20 Panamanians
were killed. Although Presidents Eisenhower, Kennedy, Johnson, Nixon, and Ford had worked toward a new, fairer treaty
with Panama, Americans and their representatives in Congress staunchly resisted those efforts, afraid of losing control over the vital passageway.

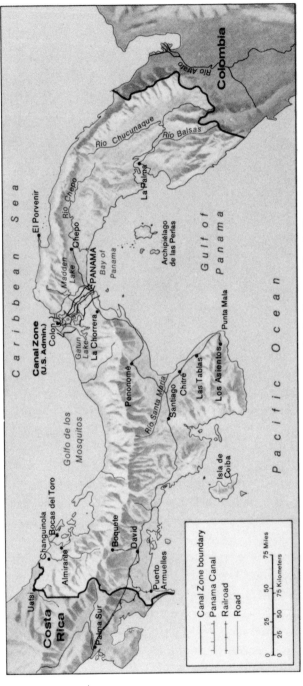

The Central American country of Panama is severed at its waist by the Panama Canal. The canal saves ships many days of difficult, dangerous travel by eliminating the need to sail the stormy waters off Cape Horn, the southernmost tip of South America. (Library of Congress.)

Carter was convinced that justice required the United States to finally give up some of its control of the Canal Zone. It was "the right thing to do," he said. National Security Advisor Brzezinski later said that, for Jimmy, the issue

> . . . represented the ideal fusion of morality and politics: he was doing something good for peace, responding to the passionate desires of a small nation, and yet helping the long-range U.S. national interest.

Jimmy also said later that the fight for a new treaty with Panama was the most difficult political battle he had ever faced.

Two New Treaties

Within two weeks after Carter was sworn in as President, meetings began between U.S. and Panamanian negotiators. By August of 1977, two treaties had been written. One returned most of the Canal Zone to Panama and allowed it to help operate the canal. The United States retained control over canal operations and the right to defend the canal with its forces until 1999, when all American forces would be withdrawn. The second treaty gave the United States the permanent right to defend the canal and to send warships through it.

On September 7, 1977, in an elaborate, televised ceremony attended by 18 heads of state, President Carter and Panamanian leader General Omar Torrijos signed the two treaties. However, it was too late that year for the Senate to act on ratifying the controversial treaties. This gave Jimmy time to conduct his biggest lobbying effort yet, with the next congressional session in mind. That fall, he invited hundreds of newspaper editors, college presidents, political leaders, and other influential people to the White House for personal briefings. Sometimes he asked in the Joint Chiefs of Staff, whose impressive military uniforms helped soothe the guests' fears. And State Department representatives made more than 1,500 appearances throughout the nation to explain the treaties.

The Fight for Ratification

Opposition to the treaties was led by former California Governor Ronald Reagan, along with conservative Republican Senators Jesse Helms of North Carolina, Orrin Hatch of Utah, and Strom Thurmond of South Carolina. However, other conservative leaders, such as William F. Buckley, spoke out in favor of ratification.

Before the Senate debates on ratification started in February 1978, about 45 senators heeded Carter's urging and went down to Panama to meet with General Torrijos, talk to Canal Zone residents, and see the canal for themselves. Many came back prepared to support ratification.

Jimmy kept a large notebook on his desk with a section for each senator. He wrote down every report or rumor about how each undecided senator might be leaning. He answered every question senators asked about the canal or the treaties. He tried to convert their advisors and friends, hoping that they, in turn, would convert the senators. He met with all 100 senators, most of them privately. Former President Ford even pitched in to call some undecided Republicans. And former Secretary of State Henry Kissinger also endorsed the treaties.

Some senators, however, were being swayed by antitreaty mail that they were getting from their constituents. Robert Byrd of West Virginia, the Democratic majority leader in the Senate, urged them to be brave, saying that "if you went by public-opinion polls and telephone calls or the volume of mail, you could replace senators with an adding machine or a set of scales!"

The Senate Approves

Carter's work paid off. When the treaties were signed in September 1977, fewer than 30 senators had committed themselves to ratification. By the end of November there had been 45, and by the spring of 1978 there were 48. In August 1977, nearly 80 percent of Americans objected to "giving up" the canal; by the time the treaties were signed, only 46 percent did. Two separate polls showed that twice as many people favored as opposed the treaties once they understood them and stopped seeing them as yielding to Communism and cowardice.

The Panamanian people followed the Senate debates closely on radio. The issue was one of great concern to them. Massive violence by the Panamanians seemed likely if the treaties were defeated.

The Senate ratified the first treaty on March 16 and the second on April 18, 1978, both by votes of 68 to 32. Carter called it one of his proudest moments and one of the great achievements in the history of the U.S. Senate. He sent hand-written notes to all 68 senators who had voted for the treaties, thanking them for their "statesmanship and political courage." Hundreds of thousands of people cheered as President Carter and General Torrijos signed the official documents in Panama on June 16, 1978.

Finishing the Job

When he returned to the United States from Panama, Carter had no idea of what lay ahead: another 15 months of fighting with Congress over the enabling legislation (smaller laws needed to make the treaties work). To pass such legislation, Jimmy now had to lobby both the House and the Senate. He called it "an extended nightmare."

Those who had opposed the treaties now worked to prevent their implementation. They told members of the House that Torrijos was controlled by Communist forces and that the Panamanians would be blackmailing the United States for the rest of the century by threatening to destroy the canal. They also claimed Panama was giving aid to Communists in nearby Nicaragua. To hear evidence on that claim, the House had its first secret session in 150 years, with no apparent results.

Finally, however, despite the opposition, on September 27, 1979, Carter signed the enabling legislation into law. "The members of my administration and many other American leaders had risen to meet successfully one of the great legislative challenges of all time," he said later.

Chapter 10

The Rescue Attempt

Outside the White House, Jimmy Carter stood with teary eyes. Mounted policemen had fired canisters of tear gas to drive back a mob of Iranian students who were protesting a visit by the Shah of Iran to the United States. The cloud of gas had blown backwards into Jimmy's eyes. It was November 15, 1977. Later, Jimmy saw the event as a sign of things to come. In November 1979—and for 14 months afterwards—there would be tears of grief for the American hostages taken by Iranians.

CRISIS IN IRAN

Shah Mohammed Reza Pahlevi had been the ruler of Iran since 1941. The United States had always considered the Shah a friend, selling his country planes and radar devices even though he was responsible for jailing and torturing thousands of his opponents through the Iranian secret police, SAVAK. The United States depended heavily on Iran for oil.

The Shah had greatly improved employment, education, housing, transportation, and health care in his country, but his rule was strict and nonreligious. He was opposed by deeply religious Moslems who wanted a more religious government. They also hated the Shah for his dictatorship and for supposedly stealing millions of dollars from the Iranian people. During 1978, SAVAK killed several hundred demonstrators with machine-gun fire. The movement to replace the Shah became stronger.

Opposition to the Shah was led by the Ayatollah Ruhollah Khomeini, a 79-year-old religious Moslem who had been living in exile in Paris. Khomeini viciously attacked the United States, too, because it had supported the Shah.

The Shah Leaves Iran

As demonstrations grew bigger and more violent, it became clear the Shah would have to flee his country. Although the United States offered to take him in, he fled to Egypt instead on January 16, 1979. Two weeks later, on February 1, Khomeini flew into Teheran, Iran's capital, where he was greeted by hundreds of thousands of supporters.

Of the 35,000 Americans who had been living in Iran, 25,000 left after the disturbances began. The new prime minister, Medhi Bazargan, opposed the violent actions of Khomeini and his followers, who formed armed bands, arrested hundreds of people throughout Iran, and tried and executed them on the spot. But Bazargan could not control them. As Khomeini's followers grew more and more hateful toward the United States, the American government quietly urged the few remaining Americans to leave at once. Among them were about 65 people in the American embassy.

In the meantime, because the Shah was unhappy in Egypt, he and his family and staff moved to Morocco, then to the Bahamas, then to Mexico. In April 1979 he asked whether the United States was still willing to take him in. Carter stalled, worried that letting the Shah come to the United States would make Khomeini and his followers so angry that they would hurt those Americans who were still in Iran.

In October, however, it was discovered the Shah was

suffering from cancer. When some of his doctors said he could be treated only in the United States, Jimmy relented. The Shah arrived in New York City on October 22, 1979.

IRAN REACTS

Out of fear of reprisals for admitting the Shah, the American embassy in Teheran was given additional police protection. Nevertheless, huge crowds of Iranian demonstrators gathered daily in front of the embassy to hang banners and chant such slogans as "Give Us the Shah" and "The Embassy Must Be Destroyed," but they did not enter the grounds. Then, on November 4, they struck. They stormed the embassy, taking all the employees inside as hostages.

Throughout his whole life, no matter how difficult the situation, Jimmy could usually sleep at night. Now he lay awake, thinking of how to save the hostages. He called his advisors together to discuss a military rescue. They concluded that such an operation would be very difficult and should be avoided if possible. Jimmy quickly took other steps. He expelled illegal Iranian students from U.S. colleges and universities, and he forbade Iranian demonstrations on federal property. He also stopped all purchases of oil from Iran. And he issued an order preventing the Iranians from removing any of the $12 billion they had on deposit in American banks. The idea behind these actions was to put so much pressure on the Iranians that they would free the hostages.

Difficult Dealings

Carter stayed close to Washington to see if the plan would work. Although his 1980 presidential campaign was well under way and the election only a year off, he announced he would not make political appearances until the hostages were freed. Then on November 19, 1979, the Iranian militants released four women and five black men. But 52 Americans still remained in captivity.

Carter hoped it would help the hostages if the Shah left the United States now that he had finished the treatment for his cancer. But when Mexico would not take him back, he left on December 15 to live in Panama. The hostages, however, still remained imprisoned.

It was now nearly six weeks since the embassy had been taken. Every Christmas, the President throws a switch that lights up a huge tree on the White House lawn. This year, to signify the nation's sorrow over the hostages, Jimmy left the tree dark.

Following the capture of the hostages, a complicated series of meetings between Hamilton Jordan, two lawyers, and high officials of the Iranian government went on for months. At times, it looked like the hostages would be released at any moment. But time after time, complex deals to free them fell apart. There was so much confusion and conflict in the Iranian government that no one seemed to be in charge, and no progress was possible.

DISASTER IN THE DESERT

Ongoing efforts to negotiate with the Iranians during the winter of 1980 failed. Angry and frustrated, on April 11, Carter turned to his last resort: a rescue operation. Delta Force, the top-secret rescue team, would be led by Colonel Charlie Beckwith, a Georgian from the county next to Jimmy's.

On April 23, eight helicopters lifted off the aircraft carrier *Nimitz,* which was stationed in the Gulf of Oman. At about the same time, six cargo planes took off from bases in Cairo and elsewhere in the Mideast, carrying an assault team of about 95 soldiers and 90 support and flight personnel. The plan was for the helicopters and cargo planes to meet 600 miles from the *Nimitz* in a desolate stretch of desert 200 miles outside Teheran. The rescue team would then travel in five trucks into the city, storm the embassy, drive the hostages back out to the desert, and fly off in the cargo planes, leaving the helicopters behind.

Equipment Problems

On the day of the rescue attempt, dust storms were raging as the helicopter force flew to its landing spot, code-named Desert One. En route, one helicopter broke down and had to be abandoned, and another one had to return to the *Nimitz* with mechanical problems. After the remaining six helicopters arrived at Desert One, yet another broke down. Because six helicopters were needed for the mission, Beckwith recommended to Carter that the rescue attempt be cancelled. He agreed.

As a cargo plane and a helicopter were taking off to return to their bases, they collided and exploded. Eight soldiers were killed in the fiery crash, and five more were severely burned. The dead had to be left behind because of the fire's intensity. The remaining four helicopters, loaded with ammunition and explosives, fell into the hands of the Iranians. Later, an investigation concluded the failure of the rescue attempt was caused by inadequate rehearsal and poorly maintained equipment.

A second rescue attempt, using 200 specially recruited and highly trained men, was ready to proceed by September. But after the first try, the Iranians split up the hostages, holding them in several locations throughout Teheran. Their location could not be determined, so the mission never went forward.

After the botched rescue attempt, the United States broke off diplomatic relations with Iran, ordering all Iranian diplomats out of the country except those assigned to the United Nations. Then Carter and the American government had no choice but to continue to wait for the Iranians to let the hostages go. Jimmy ended his virtual confinement in the White House and returned to a more normal schedule, campaigning and traveling on the nation's business.

On September 22, Iran was invaded by neighboring Iraq. "Typically," Jimmy said, the Iranians accused him of planning the invasion.

MORE PROBLEMS

One crisis seemed to follow another. In April 1980 Fidel Castro released more than 125,000 Cubans from his country. Many of them were convicted criminals or mentally ill, and most came to the United States, settling in Florida and causing a crime wave. American immigration laws could keep out only a few.

Then there was Billy, Jimmy's younger brother, who had begun to drink heavily. After he went to Libya in 1978 with a group of Georgia businessmen, Billy was asked whether he thought his visit would cause problems with American Jews, who distrust Libya as a sworn enemy of Israel. He said, "There are a lot more Arabs than there are Jews."

Many people thought this remark was anti-Semitic (hostile towards Jews), and Billy became a focus of media attention. During July and August 1980, while Jimmy was busy campaigning for re-election, rumors and gossip spread. It was charged that Jimmy had shared secret information with Billy. However, no wrongdoing by anyone connected with the Carter administration was ever proven.

Chapter 11

Landslide

Election day—November 4, 1980—marked the first anniversary of the hostages' kidnapping. Television and newspapers were filled with stories about the occasion, and a wave of discouragement swept over the country.

Republican nominee Ronald W. Reagan, the governor of California from 1967 through 1975, was leading Carter in the popularity polls only a month before the election. But the gap closed almost completely by the time election day arrived. The Iranians seemed to be getting closer to releasing the Americans, and if they had, it might have saved the day for Carter. But they did not. At 8:15 P.M. in Washington, long before the polls had even closed in the West, Carter called Reagan to offer his congratulations.

Reagan had won by a landslide. He carried 44 states to Carter's 6 (plus the District of Columbia), won 50.8 percent of the popular vote to Carter's 41 percent, and received 489 of the 538 electoral votes. In a spillover of their rejection of Carter, voters gave the Republicans control of the Senate after 26 years of Democratic rule, more than 30 seats in the House, and control of four additional governorships.

The meaning of this drastic shift toward the Republicans is still unclear. But what it meant to Jimmy Carter was very clear indeed: his services were no longer required by the American people.

THE ELECTION

In the primary elections, Jimmy had been challenged unsuccessfully by Massachusetts Senator Edward M. Kennedy and won the Democratic nomination. In his campaign against Reagan, Jimmy focused—just as he always had—on himself as a person and on the ideas he stood for. Reagan, on the other hand, appealed to voters more on the basis of issues.

Reagan's positions on the issues were quite different from Carter's. He favored more defense spending and more nuclear weapons, and he opposed the SALT II treaty. He also favored Taiwan over mainland China, had opposed normalization of relations with China, and had fought the Panama Canal treaties.

Reagan paid special attention to the economy and Americans' personal well-being, asking them at the end of a television debate with Jimmy:

> . . . Are you better off than you were four years ago? Is it easier for you to go and buy things in the stores than it was four years ago? Is there more or less unemployment in the country than there was four years ago? Is America as respected throughout the world as it was? . . . If you answer all of those questions "yes," why, then, I think your choice is very obvious as to whom you will vote for. If you don't agree . . . then I could suggest another choice that you have.

Like most people, Americans dislike being told they have to sacrifice, as Jimmy had told them in his "crisis of confidence" speech. They would much rather be free from such restraints. Reagan sounded good to them.

There was a sharp contrast between Reagan's victory over Carter in 1980 and Carter's over Ford in 1976. In 1976 Jimmy had won only 50.1 percent of the popular vote compared to

Ford's 48 percent, and only 297 electoral votes to Ford's 240.
In 1980, Reagan's victory was much greater. It was a crush-
ing defeat to Jimmy and to the Democratic Party.

"It hurt me deeply," Jimmy said. "We did not anticipate
the magnitude of our defeat."

WHAT WENT WRONG?

Reagan's emphasis in a series of television debates with Carter
was well placed. A poll of more than 12,700 voters taken on
election day showed they cared most about inflation and the
economy (33 percent), followed at a great distance by jobs
and unemployment (24 percent), and at an even greater distance by the Iranian crisis (14 percent).

Other polls confirmed those results. When people were
asked what Carter's greatest failure was, 31 percent said economic issues, and only 23 percent mentioned the hostages.
People said the best thing he had done while President was
to keep the United States out of war (15 percent), create the
Mideast peace agreement (11 percent), and guide foreign
policy generally (7 percent).

Compared to Reagan, Americans thought of Carter as
being more moderate, more sympathetic to the poor, more
principled, more on the side of the average person, and more
likely to say what he believed even if it was unpopular. They
saw Reagan as a much stronger leader, more decisive and
sure of himself, and clearer about his stand on issues.

But another poll indicated that people voted more to reject Jimmy than to show their support for the conservative
positions that Reagan represented. Most said they had voted
for Reagan because "it was time for a change."

Declining Popularity

As measured by how the American people thought Jimmy was doing as President, his term had its ups and downs. Overall, the trend was downward. As his first year in office began, Jimmy was treated kindly by the media and the people. About 70 percent of Americans polled approved of him at the beginning. In comparison, Democratic Presidents Truman, Kennedy, and Johnson had scored higher, but Republicans Eisenhower, Nixon, and Ford had scored much lower. During the year, Carter's popularity sank steadily, reaching a low of about 50 percent by year's end.

It is normal for a President to lose popularity as his first year ends, but Jimmy lost it faster than usual. Experts said the drop was caused mainly by the Bert Lance affair and the government's failure to take firm, quick action on the energy crisis.

Even fewer people approved of Jimmy as his administration continued into its second year. His rating dropped steadily to 39 percent until August 1978, just before the Camp David meeting between Begin and Sadat, when it jumped sharply to 56 percent. The pollsters said it was the sharpest gain for a President in the 40 years they had been measuring popularity.

Then Jimmy's ratings sank again, quickly and steadily, reaching about 25 percent near the time he gave his "crisis of confidence" speech in July 1979. People were angry and frustrated. They blamed Jimmy for the energy problems. Not only was this rating the lowest of his administration, it was even lower than the rating President Richard Nixon received just before he resigned in 1974.

After hovering near the 25 percent level for six months, public approval of Carter's performance shot up again, doubling to 62 percent from 31 percent in the two months after the hostages were taken. When the Iranians started to attack him personally on television, Americans rallied around Jimmy, seeing him as strong yet patient in his dealings with the Iranians. Then his ratings started to fall again as 1980 began.

THE WORK GOES ON

Losing the election was a bitter disappointment for both Jimmy and Rosalynn. Rosalynn especially worried that all their work was for nothing. There was so much still to be done! Yet the voters not only had rejected Jimmy but had chosen a President "determined to run back as fast as possible in the opposite direction."

Openly upset, Rosalynn asked over and over, "How could the press have been so bad? Why didn't the people understand our goals and accomplishments?" Jimmy always hid his own deep hurt, so much so that Rosalynn would have preferred "some private wailing."

After the election, Jimmy spent hours thinking over his presidency. He concluded that he had done his best, and that his best was a good job. Because his work load was lighter, he and Rosalynn got a chance to recuperate from their campaigning by relaxing at Camp David, exercising and fishing. But then the pace picked up.

Protecting Alaska

Jimmy still had 11 weeks to serve in office. During that time, his power was less than it had been because everyone — especially Congress and foreign leaders — knew he would be leaving soon. Still, there was work to be done. Ending a struggle he had begun just after coming to office, Jimmy signed a law on December 2, 1980, protecting more than 150 million acres of land in Alaska and tripling America's wilderness area.

CLOSER TO FREEDOM

In January 1981, with the help of Algeria (the nation Iran had chosen to represent it so it would not have to talk directly with the hated United States), the President's team was getting closer to persuading the Iranians to let the hostages go. Jimmy was nearly obsessed with freeing them before he left office, when all the delicate personal relationships he and his negotiators had so carefully cultivated would be abruptly ended.

On January 16, 1980, general terms for the release of the hostages were finally worked out. They would be exchanged for $7.98 billion, which was about two-thirds of the Iranian assets in American banks that the United States had seized 10 days after the hostages were taken. Jimmy then waited for word from Algiers, the capital of Algeria, on whether the Iranians had accepted the terms.

A Deal Is Made

At about three o'clock in the morning of January 19, a call came through to the White House from Algiers. "We have a deal!" Jimmy said proudly. Three airplanes waiting in Teheran to bring the hostages home were prepared for take-off. It looked like the hostages would be freed while Jimmy was still President.

Then, for what seemed like the thousandth time, another disappointment. Problems in Iranian banks caused a delay in transferring the money from the United States to Iran. As he had done the previous night, Jimmy stayed up again all night waiting for news that the problems had been resolved. In the meantime, he and Rosalynn ate their last dinner in the White House with Vice-President Mondale and some close friends.

Finally, as the dawn broke on January 20, Jimmy's last day in the White House, the deal was completed. Again the three planes were prepared for take-off—but again they were delayed.

Free at Last

That morning, Rosalynn had to call the Oval Office twice to remind Jimmy that he had to dress for Reagan's inauguration at noon. As he left his office for the last time, Jimmy looked at himself closely in the mirror. Had the presidency really aged him that much, or was he just exhausted?

Carter and Reagan rode to the inauguration ceremonies together. Reagan was sworn in at noon. At 12:33 P.M. on January 20, 1980, the first planeload of hostages finally took off from Teheran.

CITIZEN JIMMY CARTER

After the inauguration ceremony, Jimmy, Rosalynn, Amy, and some members of Carter's White House staff climbed aboard Air Force One, the presidential plane, which President Reagan loaned Jimmy for the flight back to Plains. Upon their arrival in Plains, Jimmy's staff presented him with a farewell gift: a complete woodworking shop, already set up near the Carter Warehouse. At that moment, Hamilton Jordan thought:

> What a bizarre day this has been! Just hours ago, Jimmy Carter sat in the Oval Office, orchestrating a complex international agreement involving human lives, billions of dollars, and the honor of a great nation. And now, here we are in an old barn in south Georgia, and Carter is poring over drills and saws and screwdrivers.

Visiting the Hostages

The next morning, Jimmy and some members of his staff who had worked on the hostage crisis flew on Air Force One to Wiesbaden, West Germany, where the hostages had landed. An official warned Jimmy that the hostages had all been sub-

Flying home to Plains on Air Force One following the inaugu-
ration of Ronald Reagan on January 20, 1981. (Jimmy Carter
Library.)

jected to mental abuse, that some had been tortured, and that the group was hostile toward him because they did not know how hard he had worked to rescue them. The Iranians had told them over and over again, "The U.S. doesn't care about you; Carter doesn't care about you."

The former hostages sat in three circles of folding chairs in a big hospital room. As Jimmy entered, they rose to their feet and applauded politely. He began to walk around the room, talking to each of them. The third person he spoke to had tears in his eyes, and when Jimmy held out his hand, the man threw his arms around him. After that, each of them hugged him. Many cried.

But some of the former hostages were angry that the United States had let the Shah into the country, that their lives had been jeopardized by the rescue attempt, and that the nation's honor had been lost in gaining their freedom. Jimmy calmly and patiently explained that the Shah had required medical treatment that was available only in the United States and that the rescue attempt was a last resort. He also told them that the United States had not apologized for anything and had not returned the Shah to Iran, as the Iranians had demanded, so the country had retained its honor.

The former hostages relaxed after hearing Jimmy's explanation. The psychiatrist in charge then told Jimmy that his visit had not only been good therapy, it also served as proof that the United States had cared deeply about the plight of the hostages.

On the flight back to Plains, Hamilton Jordan glanced over at Jimmy. They had met when Jimmy was 41. Now Jimmy was 56. His boyish look had disappeared. His formerly sandy hair was gray, and worry lines showed on his face. It *had* been a rough four years.

Chapter 12

Home Again

After returning to Plains from Wiesbaden, Jimmy slept for nearly 24 hours. He had gone without sleep for three days. Then he awoke to face "an altogether new, unwanted, and potentially empty life."

It seemed his new life might be not only empty but poor. Before he had left Georgia for Washington, Jimmy had rented out his farmland and left his peanut business in Billy's hands. Now, drought and poor management had damaged both so badly that the Carters were deeply in debt. Even the ever-optimistic Jimmy asked, "Would we ever look back on this election and say losing was for the best?"

Jimmy and Rosalynn thought about moving to Atlanta, where life would be more exciting than in Plains. Amy voted for that, because she had grown up there and in Washington. But they decided instead to remain in quiet Plains, where there were people who loved them for themselves, not for whatever power or influence they might have had, and who had known their names when the rest of the world was asking, "Jimmy *who*?"

RECOVERING FROM DEFEAT

The house in Plains had been vacant for 10 years and needed a lot of work. The first project was to install a floor in the attic. The hard physical work felt good to Jimmy and

Rosalynn. It also took their minds off their emotional pain. As the first difficult days passed, Jimmy and Rosalynn had time to get to know each other again, after so many years of separate commitments. Their new life began to look more promising.

Before long, Jimmy and Rosalynn began to appreciate being free to do what they wanted when they wanted instead of having to follow a strict schedule. They could wear comfortable clothes every day. They planted a vegetable garden and walked through the woods picking blackberries and grapes that grew wild next to the trails. They also jogged and biked on the country roads and fished in their own pond. They sold the peanut business, making enough money to hold on to their farmland. Contracts to write their memoirs brought in more money.

The Daily Routine

Jimmy quickly got into a routine schedule, waking up at 5:00 each morning to work on his book. Rosalynn joined him for breakfast at 7:30, then would work on her book. Because Amy had no friends in Plains, she went off to boarding school in Atlanta.

With just the two of them at home all day every day, Jimmy and Rosalynn had to learn how to be together and apart at the same time. One day, as they continued to unwind, they laughed to realize how very important the straightness of a brick path they were making from the house to the street seemed to have become.

Soon, with a constant stream of visitors, including President Sadat, Jimmy and Rosalynn started to miss the peace and quiet they had so enjoyed at Camp David, where they had often escaped for short fishing and cross-country skiing vacations while in Washington. So they built their own retreat: a log cabin on a 20-acre lot in the wooded mountains of north Georgia, deep in a valley at the end of a long private road. Rapids and a waterfall from Turniptown Creek flow in their front yard. The creek is filled with native rainbow trout, which Jimmy loves to catch for breakfast. Jimmy built some of the furniture for the new cabin with his new woodworking tools.

DOING WHAT MATTERS

Jimmy accepted a professorship at Emory University in Atlanta and started giving classes in law, theology, business, and others in his many areas of expertise. He and Rosalynn also raised $25 million to build the Carter Presidential Center in Atlanta, which opened in October 1986. The center contains a small apartment where the Carters can stay when they are in Atlanta. It also houses a museum and 21 truckloads of documents from Jimmy's presidency. But more importantly, it hosts international conferences on topics like peace in the Mideast, U.S.–Soviet relations, and democracy in Latin America. And it serves as a quiet, secluded place where international disagreements can be worked out peaceably. The center even cosponsors a $100,000 annual prize given to those people or organizations that have been most effective at exposing and protesting human rights violations.

Through the center, the Carters started a program called "Closing the Gap," to promote research that will give people complete, accurate information on how to live longer, healthier lives. The program also studies depression, suicide, child abuse, abortion and teenage pregnancy.

The Perfect Project

For a former President, it is not easy to find a project that is exciting, controversial, inspiring, challenging, unpredictable, and international. That is why Jimmy and Rosalynn have become so involved in "Habitat for Humanity," a Georgia-based group that helps create housing for the poor and homeless. The program does not use federal or state money, and it is not charity. Owners of new apartments have to work along with volunteers and help pay the costs of restoring the old buildings that become their new homes. The program operates in at least 171 cities in the United States and in 17 foreign countries.

In August 1984, for one of their Habitat for Humanity projects, Jimmy and Rosalynn recruited a busload of volunteers from Plains and drove up to New York City to help rebuild a crumbling tenement on the lower East Side. Their hearts sank when they saw the building: six stories high with no windows, no doors, no roof, and burned, collapsing ceilings and floors. The volunteers were appalled. They resented that anyone had brought them so far to be part of such a hopeless project.

Jimmy invited the most experienced carpenters in the group to sit with him during dinner and discuss how to proceed *if* they went on with the job. Before long, they were competing with each other to give the best plan. Even Rosalynn, who had sworn not to participate because of the building's dilapidated condition, nailed down a new floor. In one week, the group finished several new apartments in the building. The Carters have also helped rehabilitate housing in Chicago, Nicaragua, and Uganda.

Traveling Far and Wide

Jimmy is also chairman of "Friendship Force," a program in 42 states and more than 40 countries (including the Soviet Union) through which individuals and families, including the Carters, visit and stay in each other's homes around the world.

Since leaving the White House, Jimmy and Rosalynn

have traveled extensively. They visited China in 1981 and have been to Japan several times. In 1983 they visited Egypt, Israel, Jordan, Lebanon, and Syria in connection with a Mideast conference at the Carter Center. Because they both speak fluent Spanish and are especially fond of the people in Central and South America, they have enjoyed visits to Brazil, Colombia, El Salvador, Mexico, and Peru. They have also visited England, New Zealand, and Australia, and in October 1985, they trekked in the mountains of Nepal for two weeks.

Leisure and Family

Though the Carters enjoy many different activities – such as skiing, bowling, wind surfing, photography, gourmet cooking, oil painting, bird-watching, and collecting old bottles and Indian arrowheads – Jimmy's favorite pastimes are fishing and hunting, just as they were when he was growing up. He has a huge library of fishing books and has fished and hunted all over the world. He also enjoys jogging but has cut back on his running to about 15 miles a week from the 40 miles a week he used to do.

Jimmy and Rosalynn love to spend time with their six grandchildren, either in Plains or at the cabin. And all 15 in the family take an annual vacation together.

THE CARTER LEGACY

By the 1980 presidential election, more than 40 percent of the American people thought Jimmy Carter was weak and indecisive. Today, many believe he was an ineffective and unsuccessful President. How could a person who had risen so quickly to the presidency fall so hard? A number of experts have written on this question.

Personal Weaknesses

One of the biggest criticisms of Jimmy Carter is that he was naive. His initial proposal in the SALT talks was so drastic that it angered the Soviets. He was also more surprised than he should have been when the Russians invaded Afghanistan. And he thought he could reorganize the federal government as easily as he had the state government of Georgia.

Of special importance was Jimmy's refusal to "act political." He was not a backslapper; he would not trade favors to get his way in Congress. Some have said that as a Democrat with a largely Democratic Congress, Jimmy should have been able to accomplish more than he did. In particular, it should not have been so difficult to pass the energy bills. Some say he had a "cold" personality and could not make enough friends in Congress to be effective. They also say his unusual "socially liberal but fiscally conservative" policies confused some Democrats, costing him their support and dividing the party.

Carter's refusal to act political was seen by some as a sign of arrogance. He deliberately set himself apart from the Washington crowd, calling himself "an outsider," and that is exactly how he was perceived. Jimmy saw such aloofness as a way of keeping his word to the American people to represent their interests, even if such behavior was politically unpopular.

Carter has also been accused of being too much of a moralist and not enough of a militarist. In other words, he would rather preach than fight—he was too soft, not powerful enough. However, there does not seem to be much truth to that accusation. The nation was at peace during his administration; he was the first President since Herbert Hoover under whom no troops died in combat. Nevertheless, during

Carter's presidency defense spending actually grew, reversing a trend of shrinking defense budgets.

But Jimmy seemed weak particularly because of Iran. Some say he should have known that the Shah's government would fall and taken steps to prevent it. If the Shah had been kept in power, the hostages never would have been seized. Others disagree with that assessment. In any case, once the hostages were seized, he did all he could. Outright military action almost certainly would have been fatal to the hostages.

A Poor Image

In politics, what *seems* to be is as important as what actually *is*. A good presidential image, both at home and abroad, is essential.

The press, however, was hard on Jimmy – much harder than it was on Reagan, for example. It hurt his image by exaggerating the importance of the Billy Carter and Bert Lance affairs. On television, Jimmy did not look good, especially in the series of debates with Reagan. Over the radio, some said, he sounded like he had won those debates. But many experts say he was not a moving, convincing speaker and never could (or even wanted to) create a convincing presidential image for himself.

Bad Luck

There is no question that bad luck played a big part in Jimmy's defeat. He certainly was not to blame for the Russian invasion of Afghanistan, which wrecked the SALT II talks, or for the flood of refugees from Cuba. No one really knows how to cure inflation. Bad luck also played a major role in the disastrous Iranian rescue mission (though, as Commander-in-Chief, he did bear ultimate responsibility for its failure). And he was victimized by the Iranians, who did not release the hostages until after the election.

Still the Bold Leader

Despite the bad luck (and some shortcomings), Jimmy Carter accomplished a great deal as President. Furthermore, what his administration achieved is more a reflection of Jimmy as a person than of the people with whom he surrounded himself, which is often the case in other presidencies.

Jimmy almost always preferred to handle difficult matters by himself rather than assigning them to some of his many advisors. In all his efforts he showed himself to be unusually bright, well organized, and hard-working, with a tremendous ability to master details. Some of his advisors criticized him for his individualistic tendencies, saying he became too caught up in details and did not use his staff wisely.

One of the outstanding qualities of Carter's presidency was his boldness, a quality he demonstrated throughout his political career. Despite the suggestion of his advisors that he should wait until his second term to push for the Panama Canal treaties and the Mideast talks, he vigorously attacked those issues anyway. Carter was anxious to accomplish what he could in the four years in office he knew he had.

Through Carter's constant pressure, the number of Jews allowed to leave the Soviet Union climbed from 14,261 in 1976 to a peak of 51,320 in 1979. It dropped to 9,447 when Jimmy's term was over and has fallen lower since then. His strong stand on human rights also unquestionably kept some other governments from harming their citizens.

Domestically, Carter was bold, too. He appointed more blacks, women, and Hispanics to federal judgeships than had all previous Presidents combined. But Jimmy's boldness also cost him. Because he took on so many and such complex domestic and foreign affairs, he quickly used up all the congressional good will he had when he took office.

A Good Man

Whatever else he was, Jimmy was an unusually decent President. He said he would not lie, and he never did. He was not only honest but genuinely compassionate, as shown by his activities since leaving office. And out of his strong love for nature, he protected a huge wilderness area in Alaska. He was, and is, a man of principle and action.

Typically, Jimmy himself feels satisfied with his presidency. "I think we did a good job," he has said. "I feel quite at ease with it. I would hope that 100 years from now, when people thought about my name they would think about peace and human rights, about keeping our nation in the forefront of the world's leadership in environmental protection."

Bibliography

Adler, Bill. *The Wit and Wisdom of Jimmy Carter.* Secaucus, N.J.: Citadel Press, 1977. An easy-to-read, chronologically organized book containing remarks, observations, and comments by Jimmy Carter on a variety of subjects.

Baker, James T. *A Southern Baptist in the White House.* Philadelphia: Westminster Press, 1977. Discusses Jimmy's religious beliefs and their influence on his presidency.

Carter, Jimmy. *An Outdoor Journal: Adventures and Reflections.* New York: Bantam Books, 1988. Carter's personal account of his fishing and hunting activities since leaving the White House, with some reflections on his presidency.

Carter, Jimmy. *Why Not the Best?* Nashville, Tenn.: Broadman Press, 1975. Jimmy's official autobiography is interesting and easy to read even if somewhat out of date.

Carter, Jimmy and Rosalynn. *Everything to Gain: Making the Most of the Rest of Your Life.* New York: Random House, 1987. Describes how the Carters have spent their time since leaving the White House.

Glad, Betty. *Jimmy Carter: In Search of the Great White House.* New York: Norton, 1980. By far the most thorough, best-researched, and best-written biography available on Jimmy Carter.

Kucharsky, David. *The Man from Plains: The Mind and Spirit of Jimmy Carter.* New York: Harper & Row, 1976. A fairly good and fairly easy biography about the former President.

Schram, Martin. *Running for President: A Journal of the Campaign.* New York: Pocket Books, 1976. An analytical but fairly easy account of Carter's campaign for the presidency in 1976.

Shogan, Robert. *Promises to Keep: Carter's First 100 Days.* New York: Crowell, 1977. Written before he left office, this book measures promises against performance during Carter's first 100 days in office.

Stroud, Kandy. *How Jimmy Won: The Victory Campaign from Plains to the White House.* New York: Morrow, 1977. Another account of Carter's presidential campaign. Fairly easy; not too analytical, with stories.

Wheeler, Leslie. *Jimmy Who?* Woodbury, N.Y.: Barron's, 1976. A good biography of Carter's life up to the time he became President.

Index